Jam Today

Jam Today

A Diary Of Cooking
With What You've Got

TOD DAVIES

EXTERMINATING ANGEL
PRESS

Portions of this book first appeared, some in different form, on the Exterminating Angel Press online magazine at **www.exterminatingangel.com**

EXTERMINATING ANGEL PRESS
"Creative Solutions for Practical Idealists"
Visit **www.exterminatingangel.com** to join the conversation
info@exterminatingangel.com

Book design by Mike Madrid

Davies, Tod, 1955-
    Jam today : a diary of cooking with what you've got /
Tod Davies.
    p. cm.
    Includes index.
    LCCN 2009902385
    ISBN-13: 978-1-935259-04-6
    ISBN-10: 1-935259-04-0

    1. Cookery. 2. Food.   I. Title.

TX652.9.D385 2009   641.5
                    QBI09-200046

Printed in The United States of America

Contents

For Alex

List of Recipes

Recipes

Foreword

"My secret intention was to teach the reader
how to cook without recipes."

—Richard Olney, in his memoir *Reflexions*

There is no jam in this book. I know that's kind of weird, given its title, and given that it's a cookbook . . . of sorts. But there it is.

The title, *Jam Today*, comes from Lewis Carroll's Alice book, *Through the Looking Glass*. Maybe you remember Alice's exchange with the Queen? Where the Queen says, "The rule is, jam to-morrow and jam yesterday—but never jam *to-day*."

And Alice objects, "It must come sometimes to 'jam today'."

Well I, along with Alice, object. Why is it always jam yesterday and jam tomorrow, but never jam today?

So the *Jam Today* cookbook is not really a cookbook, not really a memoir—it's an answer to the Queen.

It's one person cooking with what she's got, in her own neighborhood, in her own family, in her own way. And she figures the way you should be cooking is with what you've got, in your own way. Not my way, but yours.

If I could be standing in your kitchen, leaning against a counter with a glass of wine at the end of a day, watching you cook for yourself and your loved ones, and trading stories about what we both like to eat and how we like to cook it, that would be the best.

But given that we haven't figured out how to get that interactive with ideas yet, this will have to do for now. It's one person's diary of some really swell meals. It's about cooking with what you've got, for pleasure, and for your own happiness and that of the people around you. I figure if you do that, it's bound to spread out. After all, it's got to start somewhere.

Jam today, not yesterday, and don't put it off till tomorrow. Tomorrow, I reckon, will be today soon enough.

Today the kitchen. Tomorrow the world.

(*And see the* Jam Today *blog for a continuing look at what I'm cooking and eating today on the* Exterminating Angel Press *website . . .* www.exterminatingangel.com. . .)

Why I Love Food

I love food. Food is part of my everyday life—and I love my everyday life. I firmly believe that you have to be the change you want to see happen in the world. And when I look at the world around me, I think: we've forgotten how important everyday life is.

Just sitting and thinking's good. Then acting after you've had a think. Going for a walk with the dog. Sitting with a glass of wine and a friend, or a loved one, at the end of the day, talking over the events of the day, that's good too. Those are the best times I know.

Best of all, I think, is planning and serving and eating meals that I've playfully considered beforehand, and then eaten with loved ones, or alone, with satisfaction later. Those meals tie me into the place I am. I like to think about what ingredients came from where, and to know the people they come from. What I eat tells me something about myself, because of what my body says it wants each day . . . and sometimes what it tells me is surprising. Sometimes it even makes me laugh. And another reason I love food: it gives me an opportunity to say I love you to the people in my life, in a literally nourishing way.

So food's political for me. Because what you eat is who you are. And how much attention you pay to the care and feeding of the people you love—and to yourself—is direct political action. Really. Think about it. If we, each one of us, make up our world, where's the best place to start with strengthening it in virtue and wisdom and courage? If you're well fed—if you're well loved—well, that makes it easier to do just about anything. And if you have an entire population that is well fed—and well loved—and believes it can do just about anything . . . this may not be good for those who would rather lull and manipulate us into doing what they think best. But it's definitely good for us and our world.

This cookbook isn't, in any way, shape, or form, a conventional how-to book. (Though I personally love those books, and cherish an armload of them, and admire the people who researched, compiled, and wrote them—among them, the ones that immediately come to mind are Marion Cunningham's version of *The Fannie Farmer Cookbook*, Deborah Madison's *Vegetarian Cooking for Everyone*, and Mark Bittman's *The Best Recipes in the World* . . . among others.)

This cookbook isn't meant to give anyone recipes to follow to the letter, or to tell anyone how to eat, or even what to eat.

My goals for *Jam Today* are much more modest: just to say how much I like food, and like cooking it for my friends and loved ones, and how thinking about it leads me to think about all the things it's connected to in my world. And how, bit by bit, I see that I'm strengthening myself and the world around me by waking up in the morning and thinking: What do I have on hand today? What are the needs of myself and my loved ones? How am I going to provide for those needs with as much playfulness and pleasure as I can?

I figure if I do that, and then expand it out every day to include more friends, more loved ones, well, that will do as much, if not more, to help the planet than any amount of hours spent worrying or bemoaning the state of things I can't immediately change.

So instead I get cooking, and then I get eating. And, while I'm at it, I get having a good time. It's fun, it's easy, and I'm absolutely convinced it's taking direct action toward a better world.

Best of all, anyone can do the same.

Eating Alone

I love to cook for just myself. That's when I get the real entertainment value out of thinking: what exactly do I have in the house and what exactly out of that do I feel like eating? I have a huge oval platter that I have these solitary meals upon—and the dog always likes them because, with my Vegetarian Husband gone, it's likely he's going to end up with a bit of meat at the end of them.

While, as MFK Fisher observes, there are few greater pleasures than dining with One, dining alone has its own satisfactions, its own silences and triumphs and downright wallowings in the first person.

Some things I've discovered on these solitary wallowings: I'll want different things at different times. Some nights I'll want a lot of carbos—fettuccine alfredo with lots of parsley. Some nights I'll want lots of vegetables—chard and tomato hash. Some nights I'll want protein—pan-fried skirt steak with garlic salt, on a piece of pan-fried bread. But it's never the same two nights running. It's as if my body's always calibrating itself, adding something missing here, holding back on something too present there.

I have a blast engaging in this dialogue with my body. I like my body telling me its likes and dislikes. Why should I ignore it when I listen with great interest to the similar words of my friends? In the end, my body is the friend I'm going to depend on the most.

The other night, I had a couple of egg whites left over from dinner the night before. (I'd made a roast chicken/ bacon/tomato

1

club sandwich, and some homemade mayonnaise to go on the bread. The first mayonnaise broke down into an oily mess—it happens sometimes—so I poured it into a measuring cup, cleaned out the mortar, broke another egg yolk in, and added the broken mayonnaise drop by drop, beating all the while. It came out perfectly the second time.) I also had some raw Swiss cheese.

So I made a puffy omelet:

1. I turned the oven on to 400°.
2. Smeared a small skillet with butter.
3. Beat three egg whites until "stiff but not dry" (this means they stand up in peaks, all shiny, in the bowl).
4. Beat the egg yolk till it was thick and lemony colored.
5. Added salt and pepper to the egg yolk.
6. (Meanwhile, I'm heating the pan over low heat.)
7. Chopped a scallion.
8. Grated the cheese.
9. I stirred a spoonful of the whites into the yolk . . . very gently.
10. Then I folded the yolk mixture into the remaining whites . . . also very gently.

When the pan was hot, I poured the egg mixture in, smoothed the top with a spatula, and cooked it over low heat until it was puffy looking and started to smell eggy. Then I sprinkled the cheese and scallion on top and put it in the 400° oven for 4 minutes. Waited for the cheese to melt and the top to look done.

(While this was going on, I boiled a piece of corn.)

When the omelet was done, I put it on top of some chopped greens from the garden, and had the corn on the side. Glass of red wine. Read Diana Kennedy's *My Mexico* during.

A very nice evening.

The night after that, as I recall, I dined on popcorn with grated Parmesan and garlic salt. I ate it from a cobalt blue glazed bowl, sitting on the deck with my feet up on the rails, watching the bats in the hot evening air. For a vegetable—I felt I needed one—I drank a glass of spicy tomato juice . . . and then some chocolate and dried apricots after . . . that's what I felt like . . .

Then there are the nights when I've spent the day wrestling with an alienating technology.

There's nothing like technological alienation to put me off my food. Wrestling with computers, or automobiles, or even just trying to set my cordless phone to the ring tone I want. Whenever I have to deal with any of these distasteful tasks . . . and me, I'd rather learn how to churn butter than how to set up virtual links . . . I find I can hardly think about food at all—which means I am as near psychosis as I ever get.

But still, you know, even then, food is my great solace. Not eating it. (Everything tastes like balsa wood when some nice man—no matter how patient—is trying to get you to understand computer code FOR THE FIRST TIME.) I mean thinking about food. Planning it.

Which leads me to another point. Sometimes, in groups of my

more rigorously activist friends, when I dreamily bring up the subject of where we're to get our next meal, there spring up some . . . er . . . mutterings, is the best way I can describe it . . . that food and recipes are hardly important, are they? I mean when the world is in such bad shape, don't I think it's kind of messed up of me to think so much about food?

No. I don't.

That kind of thinking—everyday life is unimportant because I AM GOING TO SAVE THE WORLD—is, while not entirely alien to my thinking, at least something I feel strongly we should fight against. Not fight with it . . . maybe gently give it a fall or two, the same way a cat knocks its kittens around . . . but suggest something to take its place.

That something is that every moment of everyday life is what our world is made of. And if those moments are not good, are not happy, are not kind, are not intrinsically satisfying, nothing in our world is going to be either.

There can be no equivocation here. No saying, oh, I see your point about it being more important to (your activity here—make a living, make a film, build a bomb, invade a country, pursue a lawsuit, whatever) than to pay attention to what's right in front of you. No. Paying attention to what's right in front of you is what life is about. No other way.

Three times a day you have an opportunity to meditate on what your body needs and wants, and—if you're lucky—on what the bodies of your loved ones need and want. It's a constant pleasure to contemplate this and then to act on it, and then to see the inevitable happiness that descends on the household. Meal preparation is not just a domestic act, but a political act as well. It's a declaration of the importance of social happiness to the general well being.

Even when you're by yourself. Maybe even especially then.

So when I was just about run over by a tsunami of technological alienation recently, and just about to give up and go back to my earlier career choice of buggy whip manufacturer, you know what stopped the wave and made me stand right up and stare it in the eye?

A chicken liver omelet.

That's right. A chicken liver omelet. With, I must add, a pecan and blue cheese mesclun salad and one really good glass of red wine.

I had a lone chicken liver hiding in the fridge, left over from the chicken I'd roasted to see me through a couple of days of wrestling with the computer. And when I came to the kitchen that night, bleary-eyed, depressed, and strongly considering beginning a Mennonite community of one in my little alpine valley, that chicken liver was the beginnings of a stirring back to life for me. I immediately could smell it cooked with garlic and butter, cream and parsley. So I immediately cooked it with garlic and butter and cream and parsley. Then I made my salad, poured my wine and set the table. And then, setting the chicken liver aside in a bowl, I cleaned out the pan and poured in the beaten eggs for a two-egg omelet. At the right moment I added the liver, sprinkled it with a little more cream, folded the omelet, and rubbed it with a little butter.

Eating that dinner restored me to myself, and told that technological alienation to get lost. For the time being, anyway.

When Alex, also known as the Beloved Vegetarian Husband, is not at home for dinner, I usually sneak in some meat. It's a deliciously guilty pleasure, my meat eating, and I take my time about it.

The first thing I do is choose the meat. This is always the best and most organic stuff I can find and . . . this is important . . . it's always the stuff that the market is selling on special because it's near the due date. I like meat near the due date. I like it a little strong. I like it when it's more a mysterious brick brown, and not that bright red color. Meaty. And of course I like that it's a bargain. That always adds a little extra savor.

So last week, there was a lamb chop that perfectly fit that description, a sirloin chop, beautiful, well marbled, thick—marked down to about two dollars. Amazing. I tossed it in my basket, gloating. All the way home I thought about how to cook it. I always like the easiest way, so I knew I'd do something simple. Herbs? I wondered to myself. Thyme? I always have thyme. Rosemary? Well, you really have to feel like having rosemary to appreciate it, so not tonight. Marjoram? I had some in a tomato salad. Oregano?

I stopped there, tasting with my mind's palate. Fresh oregano. Very nice.

That week, by coincidence, in my quest to get rid of my Teflon pans (I don't know about you, but when they tell me that Teflon fumes kill parrots, and then say but don't worry, it won't hurt humans, all I can think is: exactly how different am I from a parrot, anyway?), I had bought a cast iron griddle pan, the kind with the black iron ridges that leave those yummy looking marks on a piece of fast grilled meat. My father always swears by cast iron pans, and he's quite right.

So when I got home right around dinnertime, there was the pan where I'd left it, seasoning itself serenely on top of the stove.

I looked at it. I looked at my beautiful little chop. I looked at the handful of oregano I'd just plucked from the garden, and at the garlic cloves and olive oil on the counter. I thought: "Aha! Nigel Slater! Aha!"

Meaning all of this looked just like a picture in his cookbook *Appetite*. So I took the book down and opened it up, and there was the perfect lamb chop sitting there on the page. As I had all the ingredients, I set to.

You know what? Nigel Slater really does tell you how to cook the perfect lamb chop. It was by far the best one I've ever eaten (and that includes the terrific chuletas de cordero at Las Eras Restaurant in the south of Spain, too).

This is how:

For each chop (about one inch thick), mash a small garlic clove with salt and pepper and some fresh herbs—thyme or oregano or rosemary or marjoram or even parsley, but FRESH—in a mortar and pestle, or just mince it all up with a knife. Add a glug or two of olive oil to make a paste. Massage this into the chop and let it sit as long or as short as you like.

Heat the ridged griddle pan over moderate heat. It's hot enough when you can put your hand over it by a couple of inches and feel the heat.

Put the chops on the grill pan. Press down on them with a spatula or tongs. Grill for about three minutes. Turn over. Grill till done the way you like it—I like rosy on the inside and grilled brown on the outside, so I grilled my chop four more minutes.

I had already steamed some shredded kale from the garden, so when I took the chop off the griddle, I just added the kale to the pan and sautéed it in the leftover lamb juices. On the plate went the lamb, a line of the kale, and a line of diced tomatoes marinated in balsamic vinegar, chopped marjoram, and a little salt. The tomato juice sloshed deliciously into the kale, but not quite into the lamb that way. Quarter of lemon on the side to squeeze over the whole at will.

Glass of Spanish Tempranillo. Ripe figs for dessert.

One of the most utterly delicious solitary dinners I've ever had.

Thank you, Nigel Slater.

This is what I call Gilding the Lily: fettuccine with cream and garlic and butter and Gorgonzola and Parmesan and Romano and parsley and toasted walnuts and . . .

It started out the way it usually does: I was cooking for myself alone, and part of the fun of that is thinking, at the end of the workday, about what I really want to eat. On the evening walk, I thought, well, fettuccine alfredo. I had a quarter pound of pasta, just enough for one, and I had a little cream, and I had some good Parmesan. Also there was a whole lot of parsley about to wilt into insignificance in the vegetable drawer; it would be good to use that up.

But when I got to the stove awhile later, a gust of deep yearning for garlic blew over me. (This happens to me a lot, actually. It's an ill wind that doesn't make me think I need more garlic.) And I had some of that pink spring garlic that's so mild and sweet.

Then when I went to get the Parmesan out, there was some Romano, and a little end of Gorgonzola that was in danger of drying out if it didn't get used soon.

I took those out. Naturally, the Gorgonzola started me thinking about my favorite salad, which involves it and toasted walnuts. I happened to have some walnut halves around. So I took them out too.

Then this is what I did:

Put the water on to boil.

Mashed five garlic cloves (just use one if you're not a garlic fanatic, or if the garlic's winter garlic) in a mortar with some pepper and a tiny bit of salt. (You could just crush the garlic if you don't have a mortar, and put it in a bowl, by the way.)

Added about ¼ cup cream to the mortar and let it sit.

Toasted the walnuts in a 300° toaster oven for five minutes (these suckers nearly always burn if you're not careful—watch them the first time, then set a timer ever after).

Chopped the walnuts on the cutting board.

Grated about an ounce each Parmesan and Romano into a bowl.

Crumbled the Gorgonzola end on the cutting board (I had about an ounce).

Chopped the parsley on the cutting board.

By this time, the water was boiling. I put the pasta on to cook— salted the water, then, when it came back to a boil, put a little oil in.

While it was cooking, put the cream/garlic/salt/pepper mixture into a small saucepan. Heated it until the cream thickened. Added a tablespoon of butter. Took it off the heat, added half the Parmesan/Romano and the crumbled Gorgonzola.

When the pasta was done, drained it, put it back in the pan, tossed it with the cream mixture, the parsley, and the toasted walnuts.

Served it with the rest of the grated cheese to sprinkle dreamily on top as I ate.

Read John Thorne while eating and was about as happy as it's possible to be.

So there I was alone with rain and snow, and slush and more snow. The fire was going, and, I couldn't help it, gentle readers (my vegan and vegetarian friends please turn discreetly away until after the main course is served), I had to have the world's best solitary steak dinner.

This was how it went.

Before dinner, by the fire:
    One glass of red wine.
    One plate of celery sticks with Gorgonzola cheese.
    One Lewis Mumford book.
Then, dinner alone at the table:
    One rib eye steak cooked so rare it was brown on the outside and just cooked rose red through . . . topped with garlic/pepper/butter and a sprinkle of Maldon salt when it came off the pan . . . all sitting

on a big piece of toasted sourdough rubbed with garlic and spread with half an avocado.

One more glass of red wine.

One Julia Child book, especially the section on Tripe (I told you vegetarians to look away, didn't I?).

Here is how to get the perfect rib eye steak for one:

First, buy a really good rib eye steak. The best are the expensive free range ones, well marbled with fat, particularly the ones that get marked down at the supermarket because they've turned a little brown.

After that, for the cooking: mash a clove of garlic in the mortar with some whole pepper, and smoosh some butter in. Refrigerate.

Heat up a cast iron pan to hot. Rub with some beef fat. Turn on the overhead fan. Throw the steak on and sear it on one side. Turn over and salt, then cook till done to your liking. (My particular liking is REALLY REALLY RARE. This is why I just sear one side and cook longer on the other. The side that cooks the longest is the one I turn right side up. This way I don't overcook the meat, and it still looks all nice and brown. I use this trick with broiled fish, too.)

Take the steak out of the pan, put onto the waiting toast spread with avocado, and scrape the garlic butter on top.

Sprinkle with salt.

Sit at the table, listen to the fire crackle, eat slowly.

Intersperse with sips of red wine.

And then sleep well.

(*For my vegan friends, who I know are looking at the above with horror and a sense of betrayal: go shred a Chinese cabbage, mix it with two grated carrots and some shredded red cabbage, if you have it. Toss it all with a dressing that's one garlic clove mashed with some pepper mixed with soy sauce, red wine vinegar, and sesame oil, in a 1 to 1 to 1 proportion (I use 2 tablespoons of each for this much salad, which will serve 4, or two with leftovers). Add a slug of chile oil. Toss again. If you have any left over, serve for lunch the next day with warm whole wheat tortillas spread with a little hoisin sauce and slivered green onions. Wrap around the salad. Eat. Be happy. The happier and better fed we are, the happier and better fed we're going to want everybody else to be, too. Or at least, that's how it should work . . .)*

I had the stomach flu for a couple of days, and I practically didn't feel like myself. Not because I couldn't eat—though in 48 hours, I only ventured one banana, and even that was a mistake—but because I couldn't think about eating. Well, I could, but the results were unfortunate and not what I would have hoped. But I did learn something interesting, which is that what's important to me is not necessarily the eating of the food, the consumption of the STUFF, but, even more, the thinking about it. Not that eating food, God knows, isn't important enough. But I discovered that turning it over in my mind, enjoying calories I'll never have to burn, composing meals that aren't quite right, or are completely right but outside of my power—thinking about it—it turns out that's really important, too.

In fact, it turns out I spend a lot of time thinking about food.

This has various reasons. It's not greediness. Not only am I a relatively moderate consumer, even abstemious at times (although I can go to town at a dim sum parlor, and once caused a Chinese waitperson to remark admiringly that I was "a really good eater"), but I just about never snack, and pretty much confine my real eating to two meals a day. It's not that I'm particularly hungry, though I am, I hope, at the proper times. It's more that food has a lot of meaning for me and stands in for a lot of other things than just its physical self. It means nourishment, sure. But it also means proper desire. It means communion with loved ones. It means my place in the scheme of things, in the food chain. It means my connection with every other human being who has the same needs and desires as I do. It means an ever-changing evolution in my concept of, literally, taste—of what's most elegant, what's most beautiful, what's best. Food for me is a real life manifestation of the abstract Good.

So when I tinker with my meals, in thought and word and deed, I'm really trying my best to understand the Good. So now I have to think of what I mean by the Good. And I think I mean: the Good is the best way for a human being to live. And I think that there is a best way. I don't mean that regional and personal rules for how to live might not differ, but underlying all of that is a basic set of principles that all human beings can discover . . . indeed, that I think all human beings are trying to discover. A basic set of values. And these values, I do believe, come from our physical selves. As far as we share physical characteristics, we share those values.

Now this does not mean that human beings do not have a spiritual life. In fact, I think my physical and my spiritual life are twined up together—that they're dinner companions, in a way. I have always had a hard time understanding why they got separated somewhere back in our history. I suppose it was inevitable. But when I read someone who gets hysterical at the thought that we, as humans, might be Body or when I read someone who gets dogmatically censorious about the idea that we might be Spirit (read religious fundamentalist for the first, and secular fundamentalists for the second), I just get puzzled. Surely it's obvious from personal experience that we are both?

It is, anyway, in my own experience. And food feeds both my physical and my spiritual selves—both those selves enjoy meeting together over a good meal, one that satisfies my inner and outer beings.

Although, when I have the stomach flu, they have to wait a day or two to sit down together. Then the most I can manage is a mug of hot apple juice mixed with water (⅓ water to ⅔ apple juice, heat gently, and sip carefully until your physical nature returns to its regular less fragile state) . . . which is not a bad recipe right there . . .

When My Vegetarian Husband goes away, I really get into the Eccentric Dinners for One. I tend to experiment with bits and pieces of the cheaper kinds of meat. Mind, by cheaper I don't mean the meat from torture animals, at 39 cents a pound, but the kinder cuts that, for whatever reason, nobody else seems to want that day. Those are the ones that get my imagination going. The bargain and the challenge—and also those cuts tend to be the most flavorful. Center cut beef shank for a one-person pot au feu. Duck gizzards and livers for a warm salad. Marrow for spreading on garlic rubbed toast, and layered with cornichons and flaked Maldon salt. Rabbit saddle roasted with a little thyme and olive oil. That kind of thing.

So when I saw a package of "pork riblets" at the Co-op marked "special today" —75 cents for about a third of a pound—I grabbed them and tossed them into the freezer against the next time I'd have a solitary dinner and some time to think about what to do with them.

This is what I did: I chunked some shallots (this could have been onions, but I'd found cheap shallots at one market and loaded up), peeled some whole garlic cloves, chunked a couple of carrots and a stalk of celery or two. Preheated my little toaster oven to 350°. (I don't like to get the big oven going for such a little pan . . . waste of energy, irritating, that . . .) Tossed the vegetables in a big bowl with the riblets cut up into smaller pieces, along with a very little bit of olive oil (the fat from the ribs was going to be enough lubrication, I reckoned, this was just to get things started), salt, ground pepper, a teaspoon of sweet smoked Spanish paprika, and a little of the Aleppo red pepper a friend had excitingly given me as a New Year's gift. When everything was nice and coated, I poured it into an earthenware dish and shoved it in the oven. I didn't need to defrost the riblets. I just cooked them a little extra time to allow for their frozen state.

About forty-five minutes later, the house smelled heavenly. (Of course, you have to really like pork products to be into this version of heaven.) I went and peered at the dish, tossed everything around to coat it all with the rendered juices from the riblets, and turned up the temperature to 400° to brown everything nicely.

Then I poured myself a glass of white wine and spread some mesclun leaves on a plate. (I've recently noticed my market calls these leaves "spring mix." Whatever the name, they're very handy to have around.) I quartered a lemon and put a wedge next to the leaves. When the ribs and vegetables were nice and browned, I piled them on the lettuce, sat down and had at it.

Gnawing on the bones was the best part, but the rest of it was satisfying, too. Light. I could have chunked potatoes in it as well, and would have if I'd had company. Then I would have used a bigger pan, obviously, and the big oven, and more vegetables, and more ribs— even the thick country style ones would have worked with this. Any variation, as long as it included pork ribs and vegetables, Spanish paprika, and a nice long bake in the oven that gave me time to sit, put up my feet, and think about my day . . .

When you're by yourself and feeling blue, it always helps to think about, prepare, and eat just exactly what you feel like eating.

In my case the solution is, more often than not, bacon and mushrooms and eggs on avocado, and a whole wheat tortilla.

Here's how:

In a medium sized skillet, I softly fry three strips of bacon (when I'm sad, I want more bacon than usual).

16

I pour myself a glass of wine and take a sip.

When the bacon's halfway done, I add to the skillet about seven to ten mushrooms thickly sliced. I turn up the heat and sauté with the bacon till browned and smelling great, and the bacon crisped to my specifications (I like it half floppy and half crisp, but you'll have your own ideas, of course).

Salt and pepper.

Meanwhile, I wrap a whole wheat tortilla in foil and preheat oven or toaster oven (better) to 350°.

I have another sip of wine.

I give the mushrooms and bacon one last stir, push to one side, carefully slide two eggs onto pan next to them (I hate it when they break) and salt these.

Then I clamp lid down, push to the back of stove off the heat, pop the wrapped tortilla into the oven, and set timer for five minutes.

A little more wine.

I slice an avocado. When the timer goes off, I pull out the tortilla, spread avocado over it. Check eggs to make sure the whites are done and the yolks still liquid. I spread the bacon and mushrooms over the avocado, top with the eggs, pour a top up into my wine glass, carry the whole thing to the table, and eat slowly, while reading a comforting book.

Suddenly, I'm feeling a whole lot better. And I hope, after you cook yourself something you want to eat and sit down and have at it, that you're feeling good, too.

Food for Friends

It's funny how satisfying it is to feed your loved ones.
There's real pleasure in thinking about their likes and dislikes, their energy levels—better after an all-vegetable dinner? Do they seem happier after a multi-course, leisurely meal?—and their all-around health. It's a daily entertainment, mulling over what's in the refrigerator, what will go harmoniously with what, what will look beautiful on the plate, what will make the after meal activities go that much smoother and more pleasantly.

And then there's the dog.

It turns out, it's almost as pleasant to feed the dog. And a lot cheaper than giving him the packaged stuff.

An acquaintance of mine has been feeding her dogs—and when I say feeding, I mean FEEDING—for years. Chicken paprika. Veal marengo. Beef bourguignon. And her dogs live forever.

I have a simpler standard, being lazier than her. But as I am also in a continual fury about waste, and as all my otherwise unused vegetable peelings, tops, scraps and stems go into the dog's food, I get a huge amount of satisfaction from feeding my dog even in the most basic way.

The easiest way is the one MFK Fisher talks about in one of her many amazing writings. ⅓, ⅓, ⅓: One pound meat, one pound starch, one pound vegetables. Easy.

This is how I do it:

One pound meat, either hand chopped or food processor ground. I use whatever is cheapest and best at the market—my Co-op sells organic beef and lamb liver trims for pretty cheap—beef kidneys, too. The other market sells ground chicken for dog food for a little more. My dog likes the liver the best. No surprise.

I brown the meat in a little fat. Then I add one pound vegetables, chopped or ground, from a bag I've been collecting them in all week. This means: all vegetable parings (carrot, celery, turnip . . . no potatoes, no onions, though). All stems from parsley and cilantro. Chard stems, if I've used the leaves. Chard leaves, if I've used the stems. I sometimes add a chopped carrot to make up the weight. In the summer, I use the green tops of vegetables from Alex's garden: turnips, beets, herbs, bolted lettuces, etc. Don't put in onions, tomatoes, or legumes—dogs don't like them. Don't add garlic. (I used to until *The National Geographic* told me it does something nasty to dog innards.) And do add any herbs you have lying around—thyme, a little rosemary (not too much), etc. Also—this is my dog feeding acquaintance's suggestion, and the dog loves it, too—add a little seaweed, crumbled, if you have it. It's got lots of trace minerals that the dog needs . . . and that you need, too.

I pour water over all of this and bring to a boil, then turn down to simmer till done. If I'm using one pound starch of something that needs a long time cooking, I add it with the water. I look for the cheapest starch at the market, which around here is either organic wheat berries or nonorganic oatmeal. The dog prefers oatmeal. The wheat berries need to be soaked, and cooked longer than the oatmeal. If the oatmeal is in flakes, it really only needs to be added for the last

15–30 minutes. (Doesn't matter if you add it at the start, though. Do whatever's easiest for you.)

Salt and pepper. Dogs love that, too.

I cook the whole thing on our woodstove in the winter—gives me another nice feeling of using energy for as many things as possible. It can cook for a longish time on a slow heat.

When everything's cooked so it's digestible, I let it cool, then put in the fridge. From there I serve it half and half with a good bagged dog food (be kind to your dog, look for one that lists actual meat as the first or second ingredient). We call this the Dog's Stodge.

You can add anything you like to this. I put in an occasional cheese rind, or the dried up bits of cheese I have left. Tortillas, bread, or pasta can make up the leftover starch weight. The dog was a big fan of a batch of Stodge I made with some boxed falafel mix someone gave me ages ago that I never figured out what to do with. The skin from smoked salmon or mackerel adds a nice smelly component that dogs really appreciate.

It's hugely satisfying to watch the dog try to lick THROUGH his bowl. Actually, to see him flop down and grunt with the most obvious extreme satisfaction and general feeling of the rightness of the dog world. That's satisfying too.

And that's just from feeding the DOG.

My neighbor, The Indigo Ray (that's what it says on her driver's license), has five acres of organic produce that she grows herself,

strictly for love. It used to be, I'd meander over there every summer day to have a look at the chard and the basil and the potatoes and the apples, the tomatoes and the . . . you get the idea. I'd come home with bags and bags of the stuff. Then, my husband got the gardening bug. I never thought this would happen. I'd always wanted a gardener husband, and when I married Alex—who appeared to spend what free time he had in airports and various technical facilities—I thought that was the end of that forlorn hope.

But no. Life is wonderful that way. Some atavistic gardening urge drove him to sit at Indigo's feet and plant his own garden, under her advice. So now I have my own source, closer to home. And we still have Indigo, which is something of a marvel. Or rather, she is.

One year the lettuce took over the garden—thank God. There's something particularly nourishing about eating fresh greens two meals a day. Alex and I both vaguely noticed that, now that we don't travel so obsessively and eat out so often, we also don't take a huge stack of multicolored vitamins anymore. This used to be the case when we spent most of our time ricocheting here and there. It's impossible to get proper nourishment when you're living in hotels and eating in restaurants. Impossible. It's all about where the food came from, how it's stored, how long it's stored . . . and maybe most important of all (I think it is the most important of all), how the people felt who prepared it for you.

I can practically tell the mood in the kitchen now by what I eat from my plate. And the mood in the kitchen at many restaurants is not only unpleasant, but downright ugly.

I thought of this the other night, at the end of dinner. We'd invited The Indigo Ray over. I always like to fuss over her, because not enough people DO fuss over her—and she deserves any amount of fuss. You should see the five acres of vegetables and the five acres of flowers, and the lawn, and the rock garden, and the Zen garden, and the iris garden, and the countless rows of strawberries . . . it's an art piece, her garden, of the most profound kind. But very few people see that. Most people just see a slightly loony older woman endlessly toiling from dawn to dusk, refusing to sell anything she grows, just perversely giving it away. Which come to think of it, is practically a working definition of a real artist. Which she is. If you've got one in your neighborhood, make sure you treasure her or him. It'll pay you back big time.

Anyway, this is what I made: an unctuous brown rice casserole with sour cream and chilies, corn kernels, and Jack and Cheddar cheese. Refried pinto beans. An avocado, tomato, jalapeno and cilantro salad. But this was the best part: I brought in a huge bowl of salad greens from the garden, shredded them, and covered every plate with a layer. Then I arranged the food on top, added a wedge of lime for each person, and served the whole with warmed corn tortillas and a choice of hot sauces. It's a pleasant dinner, because you can play with your food in a pleasant way, making endless combinations of taste according to what you feel like RIGHT THEN. It would be a nice dinner for kids—anything a little unctuous on a bed of shredded lettuce with tortillas and salsa on the side. Easy, too.

But this was the nicest. Near the end of the dinner, Indigo said, "You know what, Tod? I could eat your food blindfolded and I would still know it was your food. Because it's cooked with love."

That's about the best kind of compliment any cook can get. So it was a nice night. And I liked that bed of lettuce, too.

On nights when I'm feeling a little blue or downhearted, I really crave chicken liver pâté, which is not something everyone craves; at least, if they do, they don't know it until they see it in front of them. So the way I manage my cravings, along with feeding the Beloved Vegetarian Husband, is I put a bowl of the warm pâté on the table with cheese and pickles, sliced tomatoes and bread and butter, grapes and whatever else . . . and then he's happy, and so am I. (Although he does sneak bites of it, because chicken livers and garlic are irresistible, objectively speaking.)

Here's how to make it:

For a good mound of the pâté, take 1 lb. organic chicken livers. Cut the big ones in half, get rid of any membranes and bitter looking green spots. Chop a lot of garlic (you knew I was going to say that, didn't you?), a couple of scallions, and a heap of parsley. Heat a big dollop of butter and a splash of olive oil in a wide pan—wide enough so the chicken livers brown and don't steam. When the butter and oil sizzle, dump the chicken livers in, followed shortly by the rest of the ingredients. Turn the livers, mashing them with a fork or a spatula as you do. Salt. Salt is good here. Keep turning till the livers are a little browned. Then add a little hit of something sharp—white wine, red wine, lemon juice, sherry vinegar—just to liven things up. Let that cook till the juice cooks away. Keep mashing those livers. At the last minute, if you have some, add some cream. That's nice. It'll cook away fast.

Turn off the heat. If you've mashed the livers enough, you can just pile them in a bowl and eat them on toast. If not, dump them on the cutting board, and chop, THEN pile them in a bowl and etc.

Have a glass of nice red wine.

I gave a birthday party for a friend the other night, and made a pot au feu that simmered for hours on the woodstove. The cross rib roast that went into the broth didn't have any bones on it, and as I am a flavor/bone freak, I bought a batch of marrow bones to add to the soup, along with the carrots and onions and celery and parsley and thyme . . .

The dinner, at first sight, was a little odd to my guests—one of them said in a tepid voice, "Oh . . . pot roast," though I noticed she had three helpings afterward—and it's true that pot au feu is really just boiled beef with a beret . . . but still, it's superbly delicious. (Those French know something about pot roast.) And there's something really satisfying about slices of beef and crisp toast with mustard and pickles and Maldon salt.

There's something especially satisfying about marrow bones. And they're my favorite part of the whole meal.

I wasn't really surprised that only one other person except for me wanted a marrow bone with their beef, though the other guests watched with real interest as we spooned out the marrow, spread it unctuously on top of mustardy toast, laid a cornichon or two on it, sprinkled the whole with Maldon salt . . . and then ate, with sips of red wine in between bites. I did think none of them knew what they were missing. On the whole, though, it was a good thing for me, because the next night I had the leftover marrow bones reheated gently in the stock, and then served with toast, mustard, pickles, salt, etc . . . along with the leftover celeriac salad (grated celeriac tossed with heavy cream mixed with a little Dijon mustard, salt, and pepper—yum).

So here is my counsel: if you're not a vegetarian, don't be afraid of the bony and odd bits of the meat. They're the best part of the beast. I wouldn't lie to you about a thing like that. Even if it means, next time I have pot roast for a party, there aren't any leftovers for me to eat, alone but happy at the table, the very next night.

I make the Very Best Macaroni and Cheese, so when a friend, who had spent the day telling me how unhappy she is, didn't want me to make it for her, between that and being unable to tell her how to be happy, even if only for that moment, she filled me so full of frustration I could have screamed. But I didn't want to hurt her feelings, and, more than that, I didn't want to chase her away. So I didn't scream. I listened. And tried to be patient.

She told me how she hated cooking. How she hated cooking for her kids. How she bought everything readymade and frozen, and how that was getting too expensive. How much sugar they all ate.

"You should try to get the kids off white sugar. It's actually poison—like a drug."

"Oh, yeah," she said laughing, as she put a Diet Coke she'd brought for herself into my refrigerator (where it would stay, after she left, till Alex threw it out—and he mused, "Is there something we could clean with this stuff? It's like solvent, you know . . . if the car still had spark plugs we could use it for that"). "Stop my kids eating sugar? Why, they must eat it five times a day!"

More, probably—if it's true she gives them everything readymade.

The more I heard, the more I wanted to scream. Hating to cook for your family—it's a sign of depression. It's like hating to give them a kiss in the morning. It's a sign there's something wrong. And the sugar? That's something wrong. There's a reason we're obese as a nation, and we're not feeling fed. Sugar use demands sugar use, and it does this by leaving a part of you feeling unsatisfied. You eat and you eat and you eat, but you never get enough of what you need. A little bit like our wistful consumer society, come to think of it.

"Want me to cook you my macaroni and cheese?" I said hopefully. "I know it sounds boring, but it's really . . . "

She was polite about it, but I could see she wasn't interested. It was only macaroni and cheese, after all—you can get that out of a box.

So to soothe my frustrated soul, the night after she'd gone, I made that macaroni and cheese, for me and the Beloved Husband. And it really is the best macaroni and cheese. The best macaroni and cheese, mind you, is defined as the macaroni and cheese that you have refined over the years to your and your loved ones' tastes, so that when you make it, everyone at the table gives a sigh of pure delight. Your recipe may not be mine, but it will be just as much the best, as long as it wasn't thrown together out of a damn packet, with margarine and skim milk added, then served at a counter with paper napkins, and everyone looking at the clock to get out in time for piano or judo, gymnastics or ballet lessons, bolted down before the ice milk and Ho-Hos. As long as it wasn't that, it will be just divine.

This one's mine:

(This is for two really hungry people who want to feel full, or for four moderate eaters, or for two adults and two children with a little left over for lunch the next day. For more, just double the recipe.)

1) Boil ½ pound of whole wheat penne or fusilli till al dente. Drain and pour into a buttered wide and low baking dish. (It doesn't matter what shape or size; the main thing is to get as much surface area as you like for the browned cheese top.)

2) While that's happening, in a saucepan, melt 4 tablespoons butter. Add 4 tablespoons flour—either white or whole wheat. Cook gently for about fifteen minutes. Don't brown—you're just trying to get the raw taste out of the flour. Then add, again gently, 2 cups of whole milk. Add it bit by bit, not in a big splash at once, and stir... still gently...as it thickens. Let this simmer. Let it get nice and thick.

3) Grate two tightly packed cups of Cheddar cheese. The quality of this cheese is important. (Quality, mind you, not the expense . . . A lot of times the local Cheddar, much cheaper than the import, is less

money and hugely more flavorful.) I use Tillamook sharp Cheddar that I buy by the two-pound log.

4) Add a heaping tablespoon of Dijon type mustard to the simmering sauce. Add a couple of hefty slugs of Tabasco or similar hot sauce. Don't stint on this. You won't taste the heat, but it'll bring out the flavor of the cheese like magic. Then stir in the cheese and stir (still gently—see the trend here?) till it melts. Taste. Does it need salt? If so, add at will.

5) Then, if you've got it, pour in a ¼ cup of cream. You don't need this, but it adds that little extra bit of unction that says Best Macaroni and Cheese.

6) Mix the sauce with the pasta in the baking dish. Grate a little more Cheddar, and sprinkle on top. Add paprika for color, if you like it.

You can let this sit as long before final baking as you like. Put it in the fridge, if you've done it early (but don't forget to either take it out and let it come back to room temp, or bake it longer to make up for the refrigerator chill, if you do). It's a very easygoing macaroni and cheese, this.

Bake at 350° for half an hour, till the top is browned and crusty round the edges, and the sauce is bubbling. Serve right away. Red pepper flakes or more pepper sauce for those who like it.

This is best with a green salad, or one of sliced celery mixed with a strong mustard vinaigrette. I actually like it best with the celery—in which case, a garlic clove mashed in with the dressing, and a good amount of fresh ground black pepper, is absolutely required.

A glass of beer or of deep red wine for the adults. And for the children—so I've been told—a glass of unfiltered apple juice with this is really very nice.

My brother John called to get advice on how to cook my mother's soy sauce baked chicken. This was a favorite childhood dish in our house—I can still remember vividly the joy of scraping up the oily burnt soy saucey bits off the bottom of the pan when nobody was looking. All of us kids were sure it was the one heritage recipe our relentlessly American mother had brought from her Asian homeland, at least until I found it one day in James Beard's *American Cookery*. It turns out to have been one of those newlywed wives' standards of the Fifties, a darling of the women's magazines.

(Which left as our one heritage dish a completely delicious, ghastly looking, politically incorrect stale white bread and hamburger meat canapé called Cavalho Cancado, which translates, unappetizingly enough, as Tired Horses . . . it sounds horrible, but is utterly wonderful, I promise . . . but more about that some other time.)

Anyway, I gave him James Beard's version, and urged the optional addition of a couple of chopped garlic cloves. It's just about a foolproof recipe—easygoing, happy to feed a couple of people or a crowd—and I called him back the next day to see how he did.

"Well . . . " There was a long pause. "I don't know what I did wrong, but it didn't taste exactly right."

I thought about that one. "Umm," I finally offered. "I forgot to mention. About that butter. Mom used Wesson oil."

"Oooohhhh." Relieved exhale. "I thought I was missing that really oily taste."

"Also, she cooked hell out of it. You can cook hell out of it, if you want. It's good that way, too."

"Yeah, I did. Only I couldn't get rid of all this liquid. I don't know what I did wrong."

"John," I said sharply as only an older sister can. "Did you buy that disgusting cheap torture chicken in the supermarket? That stuff from Arkansas?"

"Um. Yeah. That's why I wanted the recipe. There were these really cheap chicken thighs . . ."

"First of all," I went on, hating myself for my big sister briskness, but being utterly incapable of reining myself in, "they pump that stuff so full of liquid and additives to make it look plump that you can never get rid of all of the water. Second of all, you don't even want to know how they treat those chickens when they're alive, let alone when they're dead . . ."

"Stop right there!" he said with some force. "Don't TELL me about what happens to the food before I get it. I don't want to know. If you tell me what happens to the food, I'm going to have to change the way I eat."

(I paused at that one. And as my friend Rudy remarked the next day, "Well, there you have it. The American problem in one sentence.")

"Well," I said more temperately. "It'll probably taste a lot better if you spend a little more on better meat. Try to shop at that Co-op near you. They'll have made sure about their sources, and that the

31

stuff isn't jammed full of antibiotics and stuff."

"Oh, yeah," he said, sounding a little unhappy. "I know. But I hate shopping there. I hate the people that shop there."

"John, they're just like your sister."

"One sister I can handle. But not an entire STORE of them."

Which made me laugh.

But to get back to the main subject, the soy sauce baked chicken recipe is a really good one—fabulous for kids. I've never met a kid, big or small, who didn't love it.

Heat the oven to 375º. Melt a couple of tablespoons of butter in a Pyrex baking dish big enough to hold all the chicken comfortably. (Best pieces for this are legs and thighs when they're on sale—the breast meat dries out too much. If the legs and thighs are attached, it's tastier to cut them into two pieces. Wings are just great this way, too.)

Now, if you like it, chop a clove or two of garlic and add to the butter. Roll the chicken pieces in the butter and drizzle soy sauce over them. (I rub the stuff onto both sides with my fingers, but if you're squeamish, you can skip that.)

Lay the chicken pieces in the pan so they're not touching each other, and shove in the oven. Baste every so often if you think of it, and drizzle more soy sauce on at will.

Cook till done to your liking—about 50 minutes for a nice browned batch of chicken, ten minutes more for the tantalizing smell of almost burnt soy sauce. I wait the whole hour myself. It won't matter if you give it a few minutes either way—this is a very forgiving dish.

Grind fresh pepper on it before bringing to the table.

Particularly good served on shredded lettuce, with some celery salad on the side. And terrific cold the next day for lunch, so make extra.

(If you want to be really nostalgic, use Wesson oil rather than butter. I don't recommend this myself, but chacun à son goût.)

If you've got people coming for dinner, and you don't want to fuss, this is, I guarantee, the fastest and most elegant dinner imaginable:

Linguine with smoked salmon and parsley.

Mesclun salad with grated Romano and artichoke hearts.

Here's how (for four people):

Put a pound of linguine or fettuccine on to cook. Heat some butter and some cream in a small pan (about 3 tablespoons of the former, a half cup of the latter). Reduce it a little. Add a splash or two of Scotch, or good Irish whiskey, and heat. Mix with pasta and as much shredded smoked salmon as you have (a half a pound is good) and a good handful of finely chopped parsley. Fresh ground pepper, no salt (salmon takes care of that). Serve in warm bowls.

Afterwards, serve the salad on the same plates to mop up what sauce is left. Use as much mesclun lettuce as you like, tossed with grated Romano or Parmesan, fresh ground pepper, no salt (cheese takes care of that), canned and drained artichoke heart quarters. Toss with vinaigrette made from a crushed garlic clove, 1 part lemon juice/ sherry vinegar, 3 parts olive oil, pepper, some of the grated cheese.

This can be on the table, start to finish, in about 20 minutes. The salad is the perfect one to follow this particular pasta.

Don't forget to light candles on the table.

Everybody has a dish that's the one you count on as foolproof for company, or for making your loved ones smile, or just for restoring your wounded self confidence after a particularly daring food improvisation that didn't come off—preferably a dish that does all three. And if everybody doesn't have such a dish, everybody should, just like everybody should have a friend who'll reassure you that you really didn't look as stupid and horrible as you thought you did, any time, night or day.

Anyway, I have such a dish in my stash of Recipes I Will Always Love, given to me many years ago, by a woman I worked for at the time who counted it as her premier Recipe She Would Always Love. We're talking thirty years since I typed (on a Smith Corona portable) the yellowing, stained, blotted out recipe I'm looking at now. I've played with it a bit over those thirty years, which is easy since it is, like all good Recipes You Will Always Love, pretty much cheerfully indestructible. The ingredients are easily had, and not very expensive. You can multiply the dish to feed a crowd. And you can make it much earlier than you cook it, and then leave it in the oven much longer after it's cooked without it or you coming to harm. And I have yet to find anyone who doesn't love to eat it as much as I do, whatever their age, sex, or income level.

It is, in short, the Ideal Recipe.

Chile Relleno Casserole. Or, as it says on my faded bit of ancient typing paper, Shirley's Chile Relleno Casserole.

This is the original recipe:

1.) Roast 2 large green peppers. Seed them. Dice into large pieces.
2.) Get about 1+ ½ 7 oz. cans Ortega green chilies, whole or diced, about 11 ounces.
3.) Grate 10 ounces Jack cheese (.63 lb.) and 10 ounces sharp Cheddar.
4.) 1 ⅓ cups of milk.
5.) In a huge, flat casserole that's been greased, spread the Jack, the peppers, the chile, the Cheddar.
6.) Beat 3 large eggs. Add the milk and ½ tsp. salt. Pour over casserole mixture. Paprika top.
7.) Bake at 350º for about 40–50 minutes.
8.) Serves 4–6 people.

Of course I fiddled with this recipe. For one thing, that little detail in #2 about the 1½ cans of chilies . . . I just use two 4-ounce cans, for a total of 8 ounces. I generally make this for only two people, which is half the recipe (this will only feed six people if you make a lot of side dishes to go with it, and they better be good side dishes too, because everybody's going to want to be the one to scrape at the empty pan with their fingers). I use one 4 ounce can for half the recipe, two cans for the whole recipe, and so on. I generally only use one egg for half the recipe. It's fine that way. And I add a few dashes of hot sauce to the custard, too.

You can make the dish up ready for the oven, and then stick it in the fridge for a good 24 hours, if you want, before baking it—as long as you add a little cooking time to make up for the chill.

I've found the longer cooking time is better than the shorter one, if you like nicely browned cheese, like I do. I have also found that, unfortunately, it is possible to leave it in at 350º for too long—it'll still taste wonderful, but the consistency begins to tend toward that of cheese leather. However you can turn off the oven when the casserole is done and leave it in for up to an hour before you serve it without too much harm—which is handy if you're having a party and it proves difficult to wrangle the guests to the table.

Here's what I generally serve with the Chile Relleno Casserole:

Refried Beans (Not) (recipe on pp. 43-45), which I scoop onto a mound of shredded lettuce on each plate.

Diced Tomato and Avocado Salad, mixed with chopped green onions, a minced chile pepper, and lots and lots of chopped cilantro. Salt. Toss this with lime juice and a little flax oil.

Warm corn tortillas.

I grate a little more cheese to put on the table in case anyone wants it for their beans, too.

And I put a group of hot sauces on the table. Also a little plate with wedges of lime.

Beer with this. Wine gets blasted out of the park.

And speaking of those peppers, there's another set of Roasted Pepper recipes that can hardly fail. There are a couple of ways to do these. Either char the peppers over a gas jet, turning them with a pair of tongs, or broil them under a heating unit, or just line them up on a roasting pan and turn the stove up to 450°, turning them over as they blacken. Then put them all in some closed container to steam—this makes them easier to skin. Skin 'em when you can without burning your fingers.

These are terrific a lot of different ways. You can slice them and serve them in their own juices, or with a little garlic and oil and lemon. If I'm going to keep them, I generally add a little olive oil to help preserve the flavor, and this way you have a lovely salad in the refrigerator that you can use as a side dish, on a sandwich, in scrambled eggs . . . If you've used the red and yellow and orange ones, the dish looks as dramatic as it tastes. Good with capers, too, come to think of it . . . And anchovies. And olives. And roasted tomatoes. And torn basil leaves. And . . . and . . .

So there's two close to infallible recipes, if you don't already have them, to add to your own hoard of yellowing bits of paper splashed all over with who knows what, from who knows how many really nice meals.

Cooking for Vegetarian
Loved Ones

I really love chard. I really love kale, too, come to think of it, and broccoli rabe, and endive and . . . well, I really love greens. Which is just as well, because greens are what the gardens around here produce in abundance. We're at 3500 feet, and already in the early spring the Beloved Vegetarian Husband's garden is burgeoning with mizuna and daikon greens, arugula and I don't know what all. The Indigo Ray's garden, even though it's at 4000, feet is always ahead of everyone else's, mainly because she's a witch. ("Don't SAY that," I can hear her yelping. "They burned me at the stake in a past life, and I'm very sensitive about it!" In any case, her way with vegetables has to involve some kind of hocus pocus.) In her garden, there's always early chard. Huge, exuberant, green leaves of chard on fleshy thick ivory stems. Chard as wide as palm fronds.

One particularly lovely May evening, Alex went over to Indigo's to collect some starts she'd grown for him, and I went too, just to admire the beginnings of her garden and sit in the low, gold sun by her pond, watching the real heron stand next to a bronze one she has planted there. And I came away with a huge armload of chard.

This is what I did with it.

If you have a pot with a steamer basket that fits into it, put water in the pot, salt, and bring to a boil.

Meanwhile, separate the chard stems from the leaves. Slice the stems. When the water boils, throw them into the pot. Cook till tender, about 5 to 7 minutes, depending.

Put the leaves in the steamer basket, fit on top of the pot, cover. Cook till leaves are done—about three minutes, depending. Take out. (You see the point of this? You only need one pot for both, and after you drain the stems, SAVE THE WATER FOR SOUP. If you don't have a pot of this kind, just gently boil the stems in any pan, saving the water after, and put the washed leaves with the water still clinging to them in a skillet and cook done . . . they'll wilt pretty efficiently that way.)

Squeeze extra moisture out of the leaves and chop.

Now, in a shallow casserole dish, toss the sliced stems and the chopped greens with a tablespoon or so of olive oil . . . enough to lubricate it, but not enough to make a greasy mess. Salt and pepper. ALSO (very important), scrape a bit of nutmeg over. (You can use already grated nutmeg if that's all you have, but I won't be happy about it. A whole nutmeg lasts forever, is easy to grate over a dish, and tastes so far superior to the stuff already prepped in jars that I don't think you should even consider the latter.)

If you have cream in the fridge, dribble some on top. Otherwise, don't worry and don't bother.

Grate some Parmesan over the whole thing. I like a lot, personally.

Fifteen minutes in a 450° oven, till brown on top.

We had this with mashed potato pancakes made with leftover garlic/olive oil mashed potatoes, and with steamed carrots tossed with chervil from the garden. I love that chervil, too. And there was something especially lovely about the fact that the chervil in the garden wouldn't last, because summer was already coming, we could feel it . . . and we hadn't had a fire in the woodstove in days . . .

I did used to make spaghetti carbonara with bacon, and it was the easiest, most comfortable, getting-home-late-dog-tired-and-hungry meal. Then I married a vegetarian. And, unwilling to give up such an easy and delicious recipe, I adapted.

Mushrooms instead of bacon, of course.

For two people (if you're Italian, or even ½ Italian, ½ Irish, this is only enough for one person):

½ pound of pasta (fettuccine, spaghetti, linguine, penne, or spirals are best for this. Whole wheat is good).

Put water onto boil. Turn oven on to lowest setting.

Slice an onion, put it in a skillet with a tablespoon or two of olive oil.

Slice a half pound of mushrooms (old ones are really good for this . . . they don't look so great, which doesn't matter for this dish, and they taste better. I use the just-about-to-go-off, marked-down ones from the market when I can get them).

Add them to the skillet with two crushed cloves of garlic.

Put the pasta in the boiling salted water. Cook till done.

Meanwhile, whisk a couple of eggs in a heatproof bowl large enough to hold the pasta. Grate in an ounce or two of Parmesan or

Romano cheese. Pepper heavily with freshly ground pepper. Add a little salt. Put in the warmed oven and turn off the heat (the purpose is to keep the mixture warm . . . liquid, but warm—DO NOT COOK THE EGGS).

As the pasta nears being done, throw a handful or two of frozen peas onto the mushrooms. No need to defrost. Petit pois are great for this, but regular peas are fine. Heat till cooked through—it doesn't need much time.

Salt and grind pepper atop.

Drain the done pasta and immediately throw it into the warmed bowl with the eggs and cheese. Toss everything. Toss the mushroom mixture in and mix thoroughly.

Serve in warm bowls or dishes, with dried red pepper.

This has all the basic comfort food values: Carbohydrates. Cheese. Deep flavors. Easy to cook, easy to eat. Perfect for unexpected company, especially if any of that unexpected company includes men, or children of either sex . . .

Then there are beans. Beans are great. They're delicious. They're notoriously nutritious. And they're cheap, even the organic ones. You can do about a hundred thousand things with them, all loved by women, men, and children. And they're easy to cook. Everybody groans about how long they take, but all you need is a little planning.

(It's an odd fact that you have more time if you JUST SLOW DOWN. This looks counter intuitive, but try it. Give yourself an hour—even a half hour—every day where you just sit and stare. You're saying to me—I can hear the chorus all the way here—"but I don't HAVE an hour a day to spare!" This is my point. If you do what I'm telling you, you'll have even more time than that. Because what will happen is in that hour where you're just sitting and staring, things will rearrange in your insides, and stuff like this will pop into your head: "Why was I going to drive to the dry cleaners today when I can do it Thursday on my way to little Morgan's soccer game?" Or similar. You have to give your unconscious a chance to work for you instead of against you. It wants you to be happy. It wants you to slow down. Really.)

Make a lot of beans at once. I mean, just cook them through, then freeze most of them. You've got them where you want them, then.

We eat a lot of beans in our house. Especially pinto beans and black beans, which are pretty much interchangeable—though each has its own mysterious little ways. We eat them plain in broth flavored with a lot of garlic and cilantro. We eat them layered on whole wheat or corn tortillas with shredded lettuce, grated carrot and cheese, chopped green onion, sliced avocado, and a little sour cream. (That's what we do most days, in fact.) We eat them rolled up in tortillas with cheese and raw onion. We eat them in quesadillas, next to Chile Relleno casserole, alongside baked brown rice with sour cream and chopped chile peppers. We eat them in soups, we eat them in chilies.

Probably the way we eat them the most is what I call Refried Beans (Not).

Here's how:

Buy two pounds of organic pinto beans. *(Needless to say, this can be any amount you feel like—I'm suggesting two pounds because it's a nice even number, and you probably have a pot big enough.)*

The night before you want to eat them:

Pour the beans carefully through your fingers into a colander, checking for stones, debris, etc. that probably got included in the packing of them. Rinse. Put beans into large bowl, cover with water by a couple of inches, leave to soak for up to 24 hours. (They can go longer, though not if it's hot—if the temperature's too high and you leave them too long, they'll start to ferment and taste sour.)

Next day, in the afternoon before you want to have them for dinner:

Rinse again in a colander. Put them in a big soup pot, large enough to hold them and liquid to an inch above. Fill with water. Throw in a bay leaf, some peppercorns, some unpeeled garlic cloves. No salt yet, please; that toughens them at this stage. Bring to a boil, then turn down to a simmer.

Leave them alone for an hour. Then taste. Probably not done, even if they're new harvest. But you'll start being able to tell how long they take if you taste one every so often along the way.

The easiest way to tell if they're done (but you should still taste so you really know) is to put a couple of beans on a spoon and blow on them. If the skin on the bean wrinkles up as you blow, they're ready.

They might take another half hour, or even another hour. Don't worry too much if you overcook them, though it's more useful if you don't. They'll still be fine.

When they're done, turn off the heat. You can go right to making them for dinner, or not. I've usually done all this early enough so I can let them cool on the stove.

Then, when I'm cooking dinner:

In a smaller pot, heat up some oil or fat of some kind (I use sunflower oil when cooking for vegetarians, and bacon or duck fat when cooking for carnivores). Fry a diced onion, a few minced garlic cloves, and a minced green chile (if you like spicy beans, add some of the chile's seeds, too). At the last minute, add about a teaspoon of cumin seeds and a teaspoon of oregano, just to make the flavors bloom.

Then, from the bean pot, add half of the beans and their liquid—what was about 1 pound dried. Mash them into the fat. NOW salt. Make sure you add enough.

If you've got something else going in the oven, you can bake these for as long as you like. About a half hour is good. An hour's fine, if they're very soupy to start with. Just watch them now and then. Make sure they don't dry out (if they do, don't panic . . . just add some more liquid and stir it in). Or you can just cook them gently on top of the stove till they soak up their liquid and have a texture that you like. I go for creamy and mashed, myself.

These are even better for lunch the next day, reheated with a little veggie stock or flat beer, plopped on top of a heated tortilla with various fixings. They'll keep in the refrigerator for at least a week.

As for the other half of the beans left in the bean pot, ladle them into freezer containers with their liquid (I use big yogurt containers).

45

Label with a sharpie pen. Freeze for later. You can just turn them out into the pot without defrosting. Very timesaving.

(Use the time you saved for that hour of just sitting.)

Strictly speaking, these are not actually Refried Beans, which need to be mashed into a lot of fat, and are absolutely delectable, but not something I like to eat a lot. This lighter version is much more to my own taste . . . more digestible.

Speaking of digestion, if you have trouble with beans (and you won't if you get used to eating them, but there's always that first time), try adding to the first cooking either a tablespoon of epazote, or a strip of kombu seaweed. If your market doesn't have either, try a health food store. Or you can, when you put them in the pot for the first time, bring them to a boil, let them sit an hour, pour out the water and then put them with fresh water back on to cook. This is supposed to get rid of the indigestible bits.

That's Refried Beans (Not). And what they are really best with, best of all, is Chile Relleno Casserole. That's what we like them with best. Beans on top of shredded lettuce, Chile Relleno Casserole, and Avocado/Cilantro/Chile/Green Onion/Lime salad. Salsa and extra cheese on the side. Alex usually drinks dark beer. Divine.

And speaking of Chile Relleno Casserole . . . *see recipe on page* *35.*

Then there's Gazpacho. Really. It is. Even if I don't make it in a blender . . .

So I was talking to my depressed friend, and she said again that she hated to cook, and why did I like it, anyway? I began an enthusiastic description of what I'd done that morning:

Gotten a big handful of herbs from the garden (thyme, marjoram, parsley, oregano). Put the herbs in a mortar with a couple of garlic cloves, some peppercorns, some salt, and mashed away with the pestle till they were a sludge. Then added a diced tomato, mashed that in, then squeezed in a lemon, then trickled in about a cup of olive oil.

I dumped all of that into a big bowl, rinsed out the mortar with a glass of water, added that, then added two cups of tomato juice and one more cup of water to the tomato/herb mixture. Sliced some scallions, added them. Diced three more tomatoes, added them.

Put the whole thing in the fridge to ripen till dinner.

"You didn't EAT that?" my depressed friend said in a horrified voice.

"Well, yes, I did," I said. "And actually, I remember, you used to eat it, too. It's gazpacho."

There was a pause.

"That's gazpacho?"

"That's gazpacho."

"Oh." Another pause. "I usually make mine in a blender."

It's a good thing to remember: it doesn't really matter how you get there, as long as it's fun, and it tastes good at the end.

The night before the Beloved Vegetarian Husband was supposed to leave on a fairly stressful business trip, I'd put extra care into a dinner I knew: a.) he would really, really like, and b.) would nourish him through the following days of warm white wine, crummy Indian food, and the trail mix he carries in his bag in case of emergencies.

He really likes vegetables, and his favorite dinners are when I make a lot of different little veggie dishes and arrange them appealingly on the plate. This particular night I'd done a good job, if I do say so myself, with the stuff I had in the refrigerator. Sliced potatoes baked in an earthenware casserole with cream and garlic and nutmeg, served on a bed of mesclun lettuce leaves. Asparagus roasted with butter with a wedge of lemon on the side. Roasted beets diced and tossed with walnut oil, lemon juice, and parsley. A big roasted Portobello mushroom with garlic and balsamic vinegar.

Now the advantages of this dinner are obvious. If you get the timings right, all you have to do once everything's ready for the oven is pop each dish in at the right time. So while it all cooks gently, you can sit and have a glass of something and talk with your loved one.

That's first.

Then second, like I said, it all looked terrific on the plate. I just about always use plain white plates for this reason. I like food to look like food, not like little architectural triumphs, and I like the plates to help it look as much like itself as possible. White is the best for this, in my experience.

So when we came to the table, the plates really looked lovely. The white and gold of the potatoes and cream, the dark burnished green of the asparagus, the bright yellow of the lemon wedge, the ruby colored beets, and the mahogany mushrooms.

And Alex said, "Want me to take a picture?"

He knew I was thinking about this book, and he quite rightly and generously thought it would be a good thing if he took a good load of pictures to go with the text.

"Oh, sure, thanks," I said in an unhappy sort of way. So he took the pictures and showed them to me, and they didn't look anything like the way the table looked and felt to me just then. Though they were fine pictures. I mean, he's a very good photographer. That wasn't the problem.

When we sat down to eat, we talked about why I wasn't happy with the picture taking. "I think," I said, "that it's because what I'm trying to do in writing about the food that we eat isn't to give recipes, or tell someone else how to cook."

"What is it then?"

"I think. . ." I said thoughtfully, nibbling on the end of a roasted asparagus, "I think I'm trying to support the idea that everyone should cook and eat what they have and what they like, and that the only thing they need to remember when they do is that, just like in everything else, you have to pay attention. And how on earth can you pay attention to what it is you feel like eating and feel like cooking, if there's some picture there telling you what it all should be like? How do I tell someone how to recreate this dinner: which was made with concern that you won't be eating anything pleasant with anyone pleasant for the next few days, and with a certain amount of anxious love and hope that it'll nourish you through those days? Why would anyone want to make that dinner, anyway? They'll have their own reasons for making dinner, and their own ingredients, and their own likes and dislikes. I don't see why I should pin our dinner down as if all that wasn't true. What this dinner is about is this moment in time. How could it be anything else?"

"Oh," he said laughing. "Well, if THAT'S it, of course you don't want photographs. I don't know how I'd be able to photograph that."

And then he gave another laugh. I asked what was funny, and he said, "I was just thinking that the photographs would look much better if I had time to light the food right. And I had this picture in my head of your expression if dinner was all ready and waiting to be eaten, and I had to set up lights to get the perfect shot."

I laughed at that, too. Because a choice between the perfect, immortal picture of my cuisine, and just sitting down to another ephemeral, good tasting dinner when it's hot and ready to eat? Not even a choice at all. And I can't help thinking that anyone who would choose immortality over the pleasures involved in small everyday happiness is some kind of fool. And that unfortunately, it seems to be the fools who have their say generally. Maybe because the rest of us are all at home having a nice meal. At least, I am, and I hope you are, too.

(Roasting different vegetables in the same oven, by the way, is a terrific technique for pleasing your dinner guests while keeping your brow relatively serene and your temper relatively unfrazzled. No matter what you read about the temperatures needed for the different dishes, all you really have to do is be sensible about choosing one temperature, and then

adjust the times accordingly. One really, really, really easy way to make a great dinner this way is to cut up an assortment of vegetables or leave them whole, depending on their size—chunked carrots and potatoes, celery, whole mushrooms, whole garlic cloves, whole shallots, halved tomatoes, halved fennel bulbs, etc., you get the idea—coat them in a little oil, strew some thyme branches around them, salt and pepper, cover with foil, and bake until they're all a little browned around the edges and tender and smell great. Say, 375° for an hour or so. Serve with a garlic mayonnaise and a salad, and something chocolatey for dessert. Never fails to please. And I don't need to give you a picture, because for THAT one, I'll bet you've already got the picture clear in your head . . .)

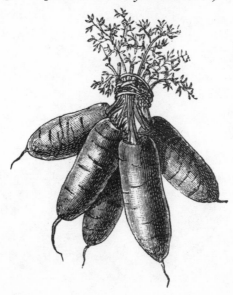

Food for Spring, Summer, Fall, and (Mostly) Winter

There is a Best Way to cook small artichokes, those little ones you can sometimes find in spring, the first ones of the season—small fat balls with purple spiky tips. Usually, I pounce on these when I see them, and make a spring stew of their trimmed hearts with whatever other baby vegetables I can find: carrots, turnips, peas, lettuce, new garlic.

But one year, the baby artichokes appeared before I could find the other newborns. It was still too early for that. And I wanted to make a warm salad of oyster mushrooms and baby kale leaves to start, followed by baked potatoes and half avocados with lemon and olive oil. So I needed to cook the artichokes some way to fit with that. I figured they'd be really good with the baked potatoes on the side, and then I found a recipe in an old cookbook—Janet Ross's *Leaves from Our Tuscan Kitchen*. She said it was the best way to cook baby artichokes, and it turns out, she was right.

Here's how:

Trim the artichokes. This is easier than it sounds. First have a bowl of water waiting. Start with one artichoke. Snap off the obviously tough outer leaves. Then, using a stainless steel or ceramic knife (carbon steel blackens artichokes for some reason), cut off the top half of the remaining leaves, down to the tender light green. Trim off any rough or black bits. Cut in quarters and toss them into the bowl of water to keep them from turning black in the air. Do this to all the artichokes.

Then, drain them, and put them in a skillet that will hold them all in a single layer. Cover with boiling water. Add a few crushed peppercorns (Ross recommends one for each artichoke), some salt, and one tablespoon olive oil for each two artichokes. Boil until the water's gone. Then add as much fresh lemon as you like—she says squeeze one for every twelve artichokes; I just spritzed on a bunch. Chopped parsley, if you like.

Easy. Good hot, good warm, good cold. My idea of a good dish all round.

Also suavely delicious and the perfect thing to serve with baked potatoes and a little white wine on the first spring night that's warm enough to do without a fire.

Sometimes too much food is just enough: at a feast, for example . . . at a wedding, or a christening, or a birthday, in fact. But sometimes too much food is just too much food, whether it's a bad habit, a lack of thought, or a terror of trying something new. (I think of this last whenever I see parents horrified at the idea of having a meal without 'protein'. Why can't you have a meal without protein? We in the States eat way too much of it; you're not going to starve your children without feeding them chicken three times a day, that's for sure.)

It's nice to think of an elegant way to have just enough. I like to do that, and then to eat it slowly, and think about how much tastier it is than all the unenjoyed rubbish I put into my mouth without thinking, at times when I don't give myself time to think.

When I do give myself enough time, though, I come up with things like nori wraps for lunch.

This is easy.

First you have leftover rice. Any kind. Brown rice, white rice, long grain, short grain. I like black Forbidden Rice, which I've often got in a bowl in the fridge because we had it with fish the night before.

Then you add diced vegetables. Whatever you've got. Cucumber's great. Scallion's nice. Radishes add color. Once I added, of all things, two parboiled sliced okra, because Alex's okra plant in the garden had produced exactly that amount. And to even it out, I added a few green beans, parboiled with the okra.

I like to add seaweed. You can use soaked wakame. Crunchy sea palm fronds. Or hijiki, just a tablespoon, soaked for 30 minutes, then tossed over high heat with soy sauce and a little sugar.

After you've got all that together, toss the whole thing with some rice vinegar—about a tablespoon for each cup of rice—and about the same amount of soy sauce. Taste and see what you like.

I spoon it out on two plates, sprinkle the whole lot with sesame seeds, add an umeboshi plum for me (Alex doesn't like them), and, on a separate plate, some fresh fruit for dessert. Fresh plums are nice.

On the table, a stack of sheets of toasted nori, some wasabi paste, and soy sauce.

Each diner mixes a little soy with a little wasabi, wraps some of the rice salad in the nori, and desultorily dips the wrap in the soy mixture, eating reflectively.

When you're finished, a light kiss bestowed on your loved one before moving on to the work of the afternoon is always nice...

Then there was that summer where it must have been about 110 degrees all week.

One of those mornings, I made noodles to have cold, Japanese style, with a sauce . . . and I made a wakame seaweed/cucumber salad, all nice and chilled in a blue bowl.

That was going to be dinner.

During the day, the temperature dropped. Neither of us felt like a cold meal anymore. So I shrugged and we had veggies from the garden and bread and cheese for dinner instead.

The temperature kept dropping. The idea of those noodles, with the sky clouded over and the rain clearing the air, seemed even less alluring the next day than it had the night before. But there they were cluttering up the refrigerator. And, plus . . . I had a craving for that seaweed/cucumber salad. I always have a craving for that seaweed/ cucumber salad, come to think of it. I don't know why.

So this is what I did for lunch: I mixed half the noodles with the salad and served it cold. Cherries for dessert.

And here's how you make the noodle salad (the seaweed/ cucumber part from a recipe in Elizabeth Andoh's *At Home with*

Japanese Cooking):

In a little saucepan, mix 4 tablespoons rice vinegar, 3 tablespoons soy sauce, and 2 teaspoons sugar. Heat it until the sugar melts. Then pour in a salad bowl and chill.

Soak one ounce of wakame seaweed in warm water for about a half hour, till it gets all huge and seaweedy. Drain. Pat dry.

Meantime, peel and halve a cucumber. Scrape out the seeds. Slice thinly. Sprinkle with a little salt and let sit for a bit. Squeeze out the liquid.

Toss the seaweed and cucumber in the salad bowl with the dressing. Chill.

Mix with a quarter pound cooked capellini. You can either use cooked and chilled noodles, or cook them fresh and refresh them with cold water. Drain and mix with the salad.

Very tasty. And, come to think of it, completely fat free. Not that you'd notice while you're eating it.

Serves two. For four, just double the amount of noodles. You'll have less seaweed and cucumber per person, but I'm willing to bet no one cares. If it seems a little dry, add a bit more soy sauce and rice vinegar. Not too much more, though.

The day after, I stir fried the other half of the noodles with some garden peas and onion and yellow squash and mushrooms, topped it with a little oyster sauce, and served it for lunch. It was still raining, and even though it was July, it felt like fall . . .

That autumn came with a bit of early winter sprinkled in, and it was so beautiful outside in the woods that I found it impossible to break away and go to town to buy groceries. So I stayed in the mountains until the last possible moment (i.e. when we were just about out of anything fresh and edible). Since the frosts came unimaginably early that year, the garden had pretty much folded up. But that's when things get interesting. I love figuring out what to do with the odds and ends that are left. It's the kind of creative activity that works the top part of your brain in a pleasant way while leaving the deeper parts free to wrestle with their own problems.

I'd been cooking some pretty eccentric things right around that time of year: eggs scrambled with white wine and garlic and tarragon served on whole wheat tortillas, with leftover salt cod and cream and potato gratin warmed up, and tomato salad on the side, for example. The aforementioned salt cod and cream and potato gratin, with baked tomatoes and braised kale from the garden; baked pears and honey for dessert. (That was a particular favorite—and a particular triumph, seeing as how it was an empty larder dinner, AND WE HAD GUESTS.) Or, kippered herrings, and a small sorrel frittata with fresh tomato sauce, and thinly sliced potatoes sautéed with garlic and onions and chilies in olive oil. I mean, you can tell these are Living Half an Hour from the Nearest Market and Too Wrapped Up at Home to Get Out Much meals.

Here's the best one we had: bucatini with sage and garlic, alongside a chopped parsley, celery leaf, tarragon, tomato, and avocado salad.

Easy. And the salad was really just figuring out if I could mix some ingredients I had just to keep from getting utterly bored with tomato salads (we had a lot of tomatoes that year; you can probably tell from the above). Alex had grown a lot of celery under the impression that they were parsley plants, and I don't know about other people's celery, but this type had a very skinny tough stem that was best for flavoring soups . . . and LOTS of leaves. So I chopped up about a bunch of parsley and a handful of celery leaves with a couple of sprigs of tarragon, and at the last minute, added a diced tomato and a diced avocado. Tossed with a mustard garlic vinaigrette (crushed clove of garlic, a bit of Dijon mustard, 1 part red wine vinegar to 3 parts olive oil, salt and pepper).

That kind of salad is really good arranged in a crescent on a plate covered otherwise by some kind of simple pasta dish . . . The vinaigrette kind of slooshes under the noodles and adds another dimension which can be very satisfying, especially if you have a glass of wine, too.

And that bucatini and sage was about the simplest thing you can imagine, and really terrific—if you like sage, which we do. (Bucatini is a long spaghetti-like pasta with a hole in its middle, and honestly if I was on a desert island and only allowed one pasta shape, that's the one I'd pick, even though I have a friend who once spent a sleepless night worrying about my choice after I'd told him so. He would choose farfalle—bowties—which I personally find depressing. So there's no accounting for tastes; you'll have your own, too.)

I slivered about twelve sage leaves (I told you we liked sage) and chopped four garlic cloves (we really like garlic, too), and while the pasta was cooking, heated it all in four tablespoons of butter till everything was just beginning to brown and sizzle. Then I tossed it with the cooked pasta and a bit of grated Romano and Parmesan. Served it with a bowl of more grated cheese at the table. Alex had beer. I had red wine.

I love eating alone in the fall. It's a time when I can really pay attention to all the changes happening all around me . . .

So . . . there was this one fall night. There were tomatoes everywhere in the garden, and little bits of different kinds of cheese left over from a weekend feeding guests. The air was crisp and cold, and I felt the need for something creamy and carbohydratey. Also, I had my usual craving for sage.

I had whole wheat penne mixed with melted butter and shredded sage, then with all the little bits of cheese . . . in this case, the end of a piece of Morbier (full fat and creamy), some domestic Gorgonzola, a tiny piece of goat cheese, what was left of the Parmesan, and a few crumbles of Salem Blue.

Also, I'd sliced a tomato, salted it, and covered it with shredded rocket from the garden, then spritzed a lemon all over, and left it to marinate while I made the pasta. I had the pasta in a bowl and ended up pouring the tomato and rocket ON TOP, which made a kind of dual temperature, decadent carbo fest, but cut by the lemon. And then, oh, I was ready to wrestle with the world once again. I always lose—when I wrestle with the world, I mean. But somehow, when I do the exercise, I don't feel I'm wasting my time.

Then last night . . . with my vegetarian husband gone, and some local farmed boneless pork ribs on sale . . . I made big chunks of carnitas . . . just cut up the ribs in cubes, tossed them with garlic salt, and roasted them at 300° for about an hour and a half. I had these on top of shredded lettuce, with fresh salsa made from the garden. I had meant to save some for lunch, but, you know, never in history have I saved some carnitas for lunch, no matter how many I make. And so it was with this batch. It took me a half an hour to get through them, with all the going back to the stove and taking JUST TWO MORE PIECES, and it was a lovely experience all around.

Just to make sure I didn't waste the heat in the oven, too, I pushed in six whole apples from Indigo's orchard, set in an earthenware dish, topped with a little crystal sugar, and a little apple juice poured around. I had three of them for breakfast this morning, reheated, and then covered with a little cream . . .

I love fall. I really do.

When it turns cold, one's thoughts turn naturally to polenta. At least, that's where my thoughts turn. Polenta (aka cornmeal mush), which sits forgotten over the warmer months, glowing gold in the grain/nut/chocolate chip drawer of my refrigerator. At the end of the summer, I start to get restless with the omelets and salads and easier dishes of the long days. The temperature drops, and I suddenly remember: Polenta and tomatoes and cheese. With a celery and aioli salad. And a glass of red wine. I remember how nice it is to sit in front of the fire while the casserole does its final cooking in the oven.

Mostly I remember how forgiving a dish it is: it'll take just about any kind of eccentric treatment, as long as you keep to a few simple rules.

You cook the polenta. You scoop the top layer off. You fill the middle with anything you like. You put the top layer back on. You cover the top layer with tomatoes, diced or sliced, or tomato sauce, flavored any way you like. Then cheese. Then dribble with oil. Back into the oven for, oh, I don't know, fifteen to thirty minutes at 350°. It has to be hot through, and smell good, but it can't have cooked so long that the cheese turns to leather (although to tell the truth, even if it has cooked that long it still tastes great).

The different steps can be as simple or difficult as I feel like making things for myself. There are all these polenta recipes which amusingly make the process as complicated as a specialty of the haute cuisine: you stir it forever with a spoon made of a certain kind of wood, always in the same direction, adding only a touch of Brittany sea salt at the exact moment the moon rises up over the horizon. Something like that.

Or—I recommend this unless you are a masochistic perfectionist with a lot of time on your hands—you can do it the somewhat slapdash way I adapt freely from a great recipe found in Paula Wolfert. The two methods taste absolutely the same, take my word for it.

Here's the easy way for about four servings (or three healthy servings with only the celery on the side, or—this is how it ends up in our house—two healthy dinner servings and two more moderate lunch servings reheated the next day): One cup of polenta mixed in a shallow baking dish with five cups of water, some salt, and a tablespoon of butter. Bake at 350° for about an hour, till kitchen smells heavenly of corn. Correct the seasoning. Give it another stir, leave it in another five minutes or so, or until it's the consistency you like. For a casserole, you want a kind of medium body—not so liquid it's drippy, but not so firm that it's better for cutting into slices and frying, either.

When it's done the way you want it, take it out of the oven, and scrape a layer off the top onto a plate. Fill the inside with a compromise between what you like and what you have . . . or rather, not a compromise, a happy marriage. Sautéed mushrooms. Sautéed onions. Sautéed mushrooms AND onions. Chopped olives. Steamed greens. Fried bacon bits. Anchovies from a can. Etc. (You get the idea.) You can put some tomato sauce on top of this layer if you like. Also some cheese is good.

Spread the scraped off polenta back on top. Then either scatter diced tomato, or overlap tomato slices, or cover with your own (or from a jar, or from a can) tomato sauce. Grated cheese over all. Dribble with olive oil. Then pop in the oven for it all to melt and meld together.

Serve with a salad and a glass of wine. If you've thought about it before, and you have them on hand, some apples or pears baked in their own dish, alongside the polenta, are nice for dessert, either with or without cream, or even ice cream.

The other night I had a skeptical look in the refrigerator and the cupboard, and assembled the possible odds and ends on the counter. This is what finally made its way into the polenta:

First, I minced a couple of cloves of garlic and a branch of sage from the garden, fried them in a tablespoon of butter, and added the whole thing to the polenta halfway through its hour long cooking time.

Then, to fill the layers, I sautéed a couple of onions in olive oil and tossed THEM with some chopped sage. I spread this on the bottom layer of the polenta, then crisscrossed a can's worth of anchovies on top. I had a little nubbin of blue cheese left that wasn't doing anything, so I crushed that into bits and scattered it. Then, thinking the whole thing was too simple, I rooted around in the cupboard and found a jar of artichoke hearts left over from who knows when. These got drained and added to the layer. Then I put the top of the polenta back on. We had a pile of late garden Roma tomatoes, so I diced them, tossed THEM with a little chopped sage, scattered them on top of the polenta, and covered the whole thing with some fresh grated Parmesan and Romano cheese. Dribbled the oil from the anchovies on top.

Baked till bubbling. I like the top browned, so I stuck the casserole under the broiler briefly till it was. Then, because I had some garlic mayo in the fridge, I tossed that with some thin sliced celery for our salad.

Red wine alongside.

We knew it was fall, all right. That was nice.

(If you don't like sage—lots of people don't—rosemary would be even nicer. And thyme is always swell, no matter what the time of year . . .)

(Also, you can double the amount of polenta easily—just double the water and butter/oil and salt, and bake for about 30 minutes longer. Very pleasant way to feed a crowd, especially with Italian sausages cooked in

the tomato sauce arranged on top.)

It happens once in awhile that I open a bottle of red wine and find I don't like it all that much. This comes from, a.) my ever-hopeful belief that I will find an inexpensive killer bottle of wine with which to gladden my evenings, and b.) the kindness of friends who tried to find that inexpensive killer bottle of wine to bring over as a gift. Anyway, when it does happen, I don't repine, and don't drink it just to not waste it, either. Instead, I make vegetable stew. This really gladdens my husband's heart, and makes him sigh with the kind of contented sigh that gladdens a wife's heart.

Especially when I make it with dumplings on top.

So this time, a bottle of Cabernet proved too undistinguished to waste on my precious one glass an evening when not on holiday ration, and I had a lot of aging mushrooms in my refrigerator (they don't spoil if you don't put them in plastic, but store them in a paper sack, or better yet, loose in a paper sack-lined refrigerator veggie bin—they just get more and more mushroomy tasting and eventually dry themselves . . . perfect for stew). Also a bunch of tomatoes that never quite ripened from the summer garden, wrapped in newspaper in vain hopes that they would—they just kind of dried out halfway to sweet, which made them a very good accent for vegetable stew.

This is what you do for four people (for two people, just make half the dumpling recipe, and have the rest of the stew for lunch later in the week . . . it's even better once it's sat awhile):

First make the base for the stew:

Mince an onion. Two garlic cloves. A diced carrot. A diced celery stalk. The stems of ½ pound of mushrooms chopped. Stew these in a tablespoon of butter and a tablespoon of oil, with a tablespoon of curry powder in a large soup pot with a good tight fitting lid (you need this for the dumplings later).

When this has cooked and smells fragrant—only a matter of ten minutes or so—dump a half bottle of red wine and the same amount of water into the pot. (This is easy to measure, since you just fill the bottle with water to the same spot where the wine was. And that way, you're halfway to rinsing the bottle for recycling.)

Add:

4 potatoes, peeled and chunked.

4 turnips, the same.

4 carrots, the same. *(Or a bunch of little carrots, as many as four people would eat.)*

4 celery stalks, cut up.

½ pound of mushroom caps thickly cut.

A few peeled whole garlic cloves *(or, if they have that little green sprout in the middle, cut in half and sprout removed).*

2 or more tomatoes diced. Or a few canned tomatoes and a little of their puree. Or both, come to think of it. *(I've added dried tomatoes before, and tomato paste—really the main point is to get a tomato accent in there somehow . . .)*

Minced stalks of a handful of parsley *(mince the leaves to*

sprinkle on top after).
A bay leaf.
A sprig of thyme.
A few peppercorns.
Salt.

Now bring to a boil, then turn down to a simmer. Simmer as long as it takes to get the veggies tender. I can't really tell you how long, since it depends on the veggies and your stove. What I CAN tell you is that you're not trying for California al dente here . . . you want those veggies so soft you can cut them with your fork without their actually falling apart on you. Trust me, it tastes better that way. (I brought mine to the boil on the stove, then moved the pot to the top shelf of the woodstove that heats the house, clapped the lid on, and figured it was done when the house began to smell of vegetable mélange. A knife poked into the largest potato confirmed this.)

At this point, take the stew off the heat and let it sit until about a half hour before dinner. It's better if you let it sit like that, and more convenient too . . . you can start it early in the day and then not have a last minute rush. Which makes it a kind of nice, unfiddly, cold weather dish for a family weekend.

When you're getting ready to eat, put the stew back on low heat and bring it to a simmer. Make the dumplings. Essentially, this is biscuit dough that you add stuff to at will— in fact, if you like, you can use store-bought biscuit dough; that'd work fine. But biscuits are so easy to make, I just throw them together myself.

Two cups of flour (I use a mix of a few tablespoons of whole wheat and the rest white flour). Mix with a good 2 teaspoons salt and 3 teaspoons baking powder. I add minced parsley and scallions here—grated cheese (especially Cheddar or Parmesan or, come to think of it, Asiago) would be good too.

Cut in four tablespoons of chilled shortening—I use butter—until the flour looks like coarse meal. Pour in ¾ cup of milk (you can pretty much use any liquid you like— yogurt's a favorite here, though I used milk this time) and stir with a fork. Add a little more milk to make the whole thing stick together nicely.

Now, back to the stew. First, stir in some frozen peas, as many as you like. (Don't worry about thawing them; I never thaw frozen peas . . . they cook so quickly you don't need to.) Bring stew back to simmer. Drop the dumpling mixture on top in balls and clap on the lid. DON'T PEEK FOR TWENTY MINUTES. They should be done then. You can tell by sticking a toothpick or skewer or similar into a dumpling and having it come out clean.

Serve in soup bowls with minced parsley lavishly sprinkled on top.

(*We had this with coleslaw mixed with garlic mayonnaise. I have a trick for this one, too, that's worth mentioning. I make the garlic mayo— aka aioli—in the food processor, then scoop out as much as I can into a bowl for use in a later meal. Then I chop up as much cabbage as I want and dump it into the mayonnaise-coated bowl. Chop it up so it mixes with what's left of the mayo. I add some sauce back if I want it more mayonnaise-y. Saves bowls and cleanup, and I have some nice garlic mayo to have with the chickpea and chard stew I have planned for later in the week.*)

You can do anything to this stew; it's very flexible. Add more potatoes. Add more anything. Change vegetables—a fennel bulb and some celeriac would make good additions. Subtract almost anything. You have to keep the onion and the mushrooms and tomatoes, though, if you want it to taste really great. If it's too thin for you, you can thicken it before adding the dumpling mix by whisking in 1 tablespoon butter mashed with 1 tablespoon flour, and bringing it back to a boil before dropping the heat down to a simmer.

It's a playful kind of dish, and good for using up all those vegetables you bought to last awhile in the fridge because you got sick of going to the market all the time in bad weather. And it tastes special, too. If you have a vegetarian husband, like mine, you get extra-added benefits, as well. Because there's nothing like a happy spouse for enlivening an evening, I find. Or, for that matter, any time.

It was really cold. And the kitchen is pretty far away from the woodstove. So the solution was to crank up the kitchen stove and leave it cranked up for a long time. And since I loathe waste in any size, shape or form, I shoved every manner of food I could into that oven and let it bake away.

Like this:

Scrubbed and pierced potatoes (we had some of these as baked potatoes for dinner; the rest I used for soup, or mashed up with cream and cheese, and stuck in a dish for baking for another dinner altogether).

Baked shredded carrots in cream (delicious that night, and the leftovers delicious warmed up for lunch, or, added to stock, made a great soup).

Mushrooms stood on their tops in a dish, drizzled with olive oil, salt and pepper, scattered in the last fifteen minutes of cooking with chopped garlic and parsley (great on their own with toast, great on top of lettuce leaves for a warm salad, great cold next day).

Baked celery and onions (chopped celery ribs and onions parboiled for two minutes, put in a buttered dish with a drizzling of oyster sauce on top—great as is, and great mixed with hot rice later for a stir fry).

Apples in a dish with an inch of apple juice. (My breakfast the rest of the week, each one reheated with, maybe, a little cream and maple syrup . . .)

And . . . most importantly . . . best of all . . .

Tomatoes. These are the winter tomatoes that I despaired of in the market but couldn't resist. And then I got them home and was depressed all over again at how they were hard like hockey pucks and white and green inside. But if there's one thing I believe in, about food and, come to think of it, everything else, it's Never Despair. So I cut them in half, laid them all out on a foil covered sheet, sprinkled them with coarse salt and nothing else, and BAKED AWAY. These can stay in as long as you like. When they come out, they'll be shriveled and black around the edges and fervently tomato-ey. You can use them for anything at that point. I chopped one up to put on the next day's lunch soup of kale and potato, and the first thing a bite of that soup said was TOMATO. Loud and clear.

Once you've filled your oven with your own version of events (whatever you've got that is calling out to be cooked) let everything bake for an hour or so—until the potatoes are ready—at 350°. And this lot can wait. I just keep an eye on it. If I'm having a good time talking with my loved one by the fire, I just turn the oven off and let everything nestle gently into edibility until the time we want to sit down at the table . . .

We had three foot of snow in a night and a day, and the power went out all over our little alpine valley.

This happens every winter. It's not that much of a worry—at least not if you behave in a sensible fashion. You can always see it coming, and get in enough supplies to last till the roads open again. Our water is gravity fed, not electric pumped, and we have a woodstove to heat the house.

In years past, I would just cook on the woodstove. But now I have a nice propane gas stove, and all the burners work in an outage just fine.

Before it got dark, I hauled out all the various lanterns and candleholders we've collected through the years, and set them up. They were a little dusty but serviceable—I didn't want to waste any of the stored hot water washing them, in case the power was out for days—. And when the sky darkened up, and we couldn't see out the windows anymore to watch the trees and the snow turn dark green gray and then blue black, I lit them all. Then they weren't just serviceable, but beautiful, too.

The room looked different then: softer, calmer . . . lovely. I will admit I was a little on the hyper alert side, making sure none of the candles were near anything that could possibly catch fire. But it was nice.

We sat there watching the fire for a while. Alex said one or two things about how the dogs must particularly like the atmosphere, since it probably mimicked the early years when their ancestors inched their way into the caves of man to get closer and closer to the center of warmth. But mostly we just sat there, drowsy and pleased. Probably I wouldn't have felt that way if the outage had gone on for, say, three days, but for that moment it was all right.

Then we got hungry. So I thought about what would be the easiest, but a little bit festive, too. Since the room was lit up like a party anyway, we might as well have one. I had to plan it, sitting there by the fire, with as much care as possible, so I could haul everything out of the refrigerator at once and keep from opening the door unnecessarily. It might have to keep things cold without electricity for a while.

Scrambled eggs, I decided. Easy to cook those in the dark. And my scrambled eggs, based on a fervent admiration for MFK Fisher's eggs, which are based on her fervent admiration for those of Brillat-Savarin, are particularly good and worth making in a dreamy, candlelit room.

I'd bought some smoked salmon for just an emergency like this—it's always good to have little luxury items packed away for when you get snowed in, or there's company dropped unexpectedly at your table, or you just feel a little blue. So it was creamy scrambled eggs with smoked salmon.

There was some leftover fennel root salad, and a little mesclun, so we'd have the eggs with a salad. I just tossed the fennel root, which marinated in a little lemon juice and olive oil, with the mesclun . . . the marinade was enough for a dressing.

And it was pretty easy to slice a few potatoes thinly and toss them in a very hot cast iron pan with some fat until they were browned, then turn them down and cook them inside, and finally toss some chopped garlic on top and mix the whole thing together. Salt and pepper.

But it was the scrambled eggs I wanted to tell you about, because they really are not what you think of when you think of scrambled eggs. At least, they aren't what I used to think of when I thought of scrambled eggs. Which were thick curdy, almost dry, bits of the inside of an omelet. Delicious in their way, but completely consigned, in my own mind at least, to breakfast, with a couple of slices of thick bacon and some toast on the side. (When I say breakfast, of course, I mean breakfast at any time of day. Sometimes you just want to eat breakfast at night. This, however, was not one of those nights.)

These scrambled eggs of mine are more a creamy amalgam, kind of to those other scrambled eggs as a tall thin mysterious woman in a simple black dress is to a thirteen-year-old soccer star. Not better. Just different. And more appropriate to an adult dinner by candlelight.

So here is how you make Creamy Eggs with Smoked Salmon and Parsley:

Put a lump of butter in a cold pan. Crack however many eggs you want directly into the pan. Five is usually the right amount for two people, but you may be more or less hungry. I generally go for two eggs a person, and one extra for the pan. Add a soupspoon of sour cream. (You can use cream, or milk, or cream cheese, or . . . you get the idea. I used sour cream because I thought it would be nice with the salmon.) Gently stir the eggs around to mix the yolks and the whites, but don't be too obsessive about it.

Now turn the heat to low under the pan. This is the dreamy part. It's going to take awhile to cook the eggs this way, but you don't want to let them get away from you, so you need to be somewhere in the vicinity to make sure they don't. I use this time to chop a lot of parsley. (I like a lot of parsley.) I add the parsley as it gets chopped to the eggs, which now have collapsed into the melting butter and sour cream. I grind some pepper in, and add a little salt—only a little, since the salmon will take care of the rest later.

Then I shred the smoked salmon. You can use as much or as little as you like. Obviously, if you don't fancy smoked salmon, or you don't have any, you can add anything else at the appropriate time. Sautéed mushrooms. Grated cheese. A can of smoked oysters, drained. Some bits of leftover ham or roast duck. Etc. With smoked salmon, you don't want to add it till the eggs have come off the fire, but those other things are nice warmed through at the tag end of the cooking.

Look at the eggs. They should just start being a creamy mass. Keep stirring them whenever you think of it. Stir from the bottom of the pan, so that you get the first cooked bits up and into the creamier layer on top.

This part can go on as long or as short as you wish. You shouldn't cook them more quickly than fifteen minutes, though, I don't think . . . at the lowest possible temperature, and stirring them so they're creamy. I've put them on a flame tamer and had them go for half an hour. If they cook too quickly, you can take them off the flame and add a little more cream to cool them down . . . or another egg, stirred in. That works, too. You can always add another egg.

When the table's set, and everything else is ready to go, and you get a little impatient, you can turn the heat up—a little—and keep stirring till the eggs are as creamy and cooked as you like. I like them very creamy, almost pourable, with maybe a little tension added in to distinguish them from just cream. You might like yours tighter. I don't know. But when they're done the way you like, take them off the heat and stir in the smoked salmon. Put them immediately on plates alongside the fennel and mesclun salad, and the potatoes. I put lemon quarters on the plates, too, if I have them. I like lemon squeezed on creamy eggs, especially when the eggs are made with smoked salmon.

Eat with a glass of white wine from the bottle you put out into the snow earlier to chill. Hope your companion is polite about the wax from the candle you used to cook by having found its way into the potatoes, and the matchstick that somehow got tossed into the salad in the dark, and enjoy.

These eggs won't let you down, I promise. And the mix of things on the plate is a perfect amalgam of flavors, as they kind of blend into each other in the shadows of the candlelight.

When it's snowing, my thoughts turn to full fat milk . . . and cream. I have endless arguments with friends about this, where they swear low fat milk has helped them diet, and I argue back that a smaller amount of full fat milk will nurture them and never harm them and help their body burn those other calories with renewed vigor. This I really do believe.

So to celebrate the snow, once in awhile for a winter dinner we have baked potatoes, and celery and onions baked with oyster sauce, and salad with blue cheese dressing . . . and carrots baked in cream. (I found the recipe in a highly underrated cookbook by Jane Sigal, *Backroad Bistros*.)

Those carrots are heaven.

This is how:

Grate about a pound and a half of carrots. Melt some butter in a skillet and cook the carrots, with a little salt, until they're not raw anymore. Then add some cream (or crème fraiche, which I've never tried, as I only ever make this dish in the States, and just try finding decent reasonably priced crème fraiche here), about half a cup, more if you're feeling blue.

Now, very important: GRATE SOME FRESH NUTMEG over

all. Put it in a buttered casserole, cover, and stick in the oven with whatever else you've got baking until caramelized. Don't undercook. It's really the best when the carrots suck all the cream in and get brown around the edges. And it's practically indestructible. It can go an hour at 375°, or even an hour at 400° . . . just give it a stir now and then, and just think, that's one or two or three helpings of your daily vegetables you're eating there. It will do you no harm at all. I promise. . .

I think I mentioned a woodstove heats our house in the mountains, and if I go away for even a few days, it's like coming home to an igloo. The only thing to do is to get the fire as close to roaring as possible, go fetch the dogs home from the neighbors, and huddle with them by the stove.

There's something quite pleasant about this (and of course it's always fun to watch your breath freeze on the air in the comfort of your own living room). Especially since being post-trip means I'm usually stuffed with too many carbohydrates, sugars, oils, and other luxuries of modern urban living.

These are all nice, don't get me wrong, but coming home to the fire makes me want to eat something more . . . elemental.

At times like these, all I want is tomato soup.

So, like this:

In a big soup pot, dump about a quart of whatever kind of broth you have (you don't have to get fussy about this; it can be chicken broth and water, or bean broth, or veggie broth, or even just water and a little wine. I used duck broth I had in the freezer left over from the kindly carcass from my Thanksgiving bird). Then dump in one of those big cans of tomatoes. Any kind you like—diced are nice here, but definitely not necessary. Then add whatever herbs you've got around. Chop some parsley. I had some fresh thyme, and, on my way out of swimming at the Y, I snipped a little piece of rosemary off the bushes that line its parking lot there, so I chopped the thyme and rosemary leaves and added those with a bay leaf. Bring to a boil. Turn down to the simmer. (If you have a woodstove, just put the pot on the upper shelf.) Cover or not as you like. I usually cover it to start, then pull the cover off halfway to let it cook down. About a half hour in, taste it and add salt. At this point, if you like, add as many minced garlic cloves as you can stand. I added five. After about an hour— again, you don't have to be fussy about this, if it tastes weak and you want it quickly, turn up the heat and cook it down while you stir; if you want to take your time, let it simmer as long as you like . . . the main thing is that it taste good, like tomato soup, in fact—taste it. Salt and pepper at will. If it's ready, heat up some receptacle and pour it in. A nice wide mouthed mug is good, and portable, too—perfect for carrying over to the fire to eat while the rest of the house slowly heats itself back up.

If you're looking to gild the lily, you can drizzle some olive oil on top. Or toast some bread and butter it and put that in the bottom of the bowl. Or spread the toast with goat cheese and dip. Or . . .

The next day I'd have it for lunch, maybe with cooked brown

rice added, or maybe with some macaroni. Then it's a whole different soup.

And I don't have to think about it too much. I can go on unpacking the images and ideas I picked up on my trip, and go on holding them up speculatively to the light. And all the while, I'm very well fed.

No muss, no fuss. Which is very nice on a winter night.

Fish

When I was at the market one day, I was happy to see a fresh whole red snapper, cheap because it was still uncleaned and unscaled. And there was some good local fennel, and some rose pink garlic. I had tomatoes at home. The sourdough bread had just been delivered to the store; it was still warm; I got some of that.

This is what we had for dinner:
> Red snapper bouillabaisse w/large amounts of garlic and fennel.
> Rouille.
> Sourdough bread.
> Goat cheese.
> Red wine.

(We had it for lunch the next day, too, but this time over garlic rubbed sourdough toast.)

To make the soup *(really more of a stew, it's so thick)*:

Chop an onion finely, stew it in olive oil to cover the bottom of a pot.

Add a chopped chile pepper if you like heat.

A diced carrot.

A sliced fennel bulb.

As much garlic, chopped, as you like.

Some chopped parsley.

While this is going on, scale and clean the whole fish. Put the head and bones and trimmings into another pot, cover with water, throw in the carrot and onion ends, some whole garlic cloves (don't need to peel them), bay leaf, fennel fronds . . . really, whatever you've got that will add flavor to the broth.

When the onion etc. is nice and stewed (don't brown), add some wine (I had some red leftover, so added that), simmer till alcohol cooks off, add plenty of diced tomato (or canned tomato). Add some saffron if you have it—it makes a difference. Bring to brisk boil; boil about 2 minutes, then cook at a brisk simmer till nice and thick and tasty. Add salt. Strain fish broth—which should taste of all the things in it by now—into the veggie pot, and cook the whole thing until it tastes really good to you. About twenty minutes to a half hour should do it. Boil it down if the broth is too thin. Taste for salt again.

Make a rouille. That's just garlic mayonnaise with saffron and red pepper added. I soak a dried pepper till it's soft enough to mash with the other stuff, and use that.

Right before you serve dinner, put out some bread and cheese—goat cheese is great. Put soup plates into oven to warm. Chop some fennel fronds to use to garnish the soup. Warn companion that it's time to light the candles and pour a couple of glasses of wine. Then add the filleted fish, cut into chunks, to the soup.

Don't go away from the stove. The fish should take about two minutes to cook.

Serve the fennel strewn soup in the warmed plates; add rouille at pleasure; if only two of you and no children to impress with manners, scrape the last of the rouille out of the mortar you made it in with the last bits of the bouillabaisse soaked and goat cheese spread bread.

We get good salmon here, which is lucky, given our landlocked status. Somehow we're on the salmon distribution trail that runs down from Alaska to the markets in California south of us, and since the fish is frozen on the boats just about as quickly as it's caught, it's the freshest we can hope for. Which is not bad at all.

Every year when the Growers' Market starts up in the spring, we have some nice woman selling frozen salmon under one of the awnings. And I pretty much buy a couple of filets every week that I can. Growers' Market day is errand day for me generally, and I don't feel much like fussing over a meal when I get home. (Although as I write this, it occurs to me that I don't much feel like fussing over a meal generally. I pretty much like a straightforward preparation during the cooking phase followed by sighs of contentment during the eating phase. Fussing doesn't enter into it.) So Tuesday dinner during salmon season is generally: a.) salmon, b.) black rice/quinoa/ or whole wheat couscous with butter and soy sauce added at will at the table, c.) appropriate vegetable and, d.) salad. Simple, easy, good to eat, good for you. Not particularly inexpensive, but a pretty good deal if you buy the fish from the nice lady selling it out of the cooler on the back of her truck at the Growers' Market.

One of my favorite ways to cook the filets is à l'unilateral, topping them after with wasabi butter. Translated, this means the fish is cooked on the skin side only, till it's nice and crispy and brown, and the salmon itself is tenderly underdone.

There are a lot of good recipes for this, but I tend to follow the counsel of Patricia Wells here. She recommends painting the skin side with some olive oil to keep it from sticking, then heating on medium heat a nonstick pan. (*In my quest to get Teflon out of my kitchen, I mostly use cast iron pans now. But I'm still too chicken when it comes to the salmon. I mean, if it sticks, then all that crispy skin—my favorite part—is lost.*)

Add a tablespoon or so of butter to the pan, let it foam and subside, put the salmon in skin side down, and cook about 6 minutes or so, till the skin is nice and crispy and etc. (I use one of those screen thingies on top of the salmon to keep the grease from sputtering all over the stove.)

Then clap a lid on it and let it steam for a minute or two, but NO LONGER, till it looks done to your liking. (This timing is for thawed salmon, though if the fish manages to make it home still frozen, I just use it that way and allow a couple of extra minutes. This makes a very rare salmon, which I happen to think is salmon at its best, but if you like your fish well done, just leave it on the fire longer. Try it my way first, though.)

Sprinkle with flaked or coarse salt. Serve with wasabi butter melting on top.

For the wasabi butter: dead simple. If you have a mortar and pestle, do like I do. Grind some whole peppercorns and salt, then add as much butter as you want, as much wasabi as you want, and a little bit of soy sauce. Mash together till well mixed. If you don't have a mortar and pestle, just mash everything, except the peppercorns, together with a fork in a bowl, and then add freshly ground pepper from the peppermill.

We had this the other night with room temperature asparagus dressed with a soy/ginger/garlic/scallion sauce left over from a tofu dinner the night before. Steamed black rice, which is particularly nice with salmon. Lemon wedges. And after, a salad tossed with a lemon/ thyme dressing with a touch of blue cheese smushed in. I don't know why, but blue cheese—just a little, anyway—always seems to go with soy sauce . . . and it's really nice after the wasabi.

As for why we have the salad after . . . sometimes we have it before, sometimes after. The real deciding factor is whether the main course needs attending to by the cook right up until it demands to be eaten. Since we have that salmon just about the minute it gets off the stove and under the melting wasabi butter, I generally have the salad on the table waiting to be tossed and served out after. (Dressing at the bottom of the bowl, crossed serving implements on top, salad leaves piled on them over the dressing . . . so the salad doesn't get all wilted and depressed while we're eating everything else.)

Also, if we've just had something that will taste good with the salad scooping what's left, it's nice to serve it on the same plates. I like that with the salmon. What's left of the wasabi butter, and the soy sauce from the asparagus, just mingles with the salad in a harmonious kind of way.

I was hardcore about getting over the stomach flu.

My first trip back to the market—shopping for my first real meal (i.e. one that didn't consist mainly of brown rice porridge)—and I found myself mooning over a bunch of live mussels. Also craving whole wheat bread, of the kind made into a whole, unsliced, rough and ready loaf. Go figure. But I really wanted those mussels, and so they went into the cart along with the bread, and some mesclun leaves for salad. I was also craving blue cheese in my salad dressing. Don't ask me why, unless it's that I permanently crave blue cheese, which is a distinct possibility.

The great thing about mussels is that they are, a.) relatively inexpensive, b.) light on the stomach, c.) incredibly fast and easy to cook. I like all these things.

So this is what I did with them, a little more than a pound unshelled, enough for us two for dinner, though you might want to have them as an appetizer if you're feeling really hungry.

First I gave them a rinse and gently lowered them into a bowl of salted cold water. You can let them sit like this for a day in the refrigerator, if you have to. You can add flour if you want them to have a little something to nosh on while they wait.

Then I warmed some olive oil and butter (just a tablespoon or so) in a big heavy casserole. I minced a little onion, a garlic clove, and a few sprigs of parsley and warmed them up in the oil until the onion was golden. I added about four chopped Roma tomatoes, a small glass of white wine, a bay leaf, a sprig of fresh thyme, a little saffron... and, discovering some Pernod in the back of my cupboard, a slosh of that. I cooked all of this pretty briskly for about fifteen minutes till it was nice and sauce-like, then tasted for salt and added a little.

Then I drained the mussels and put them in the pot with the sauce, still over a good medium flame. Clapped the cover on them.

While they cooked—these were good tiny ones, and only took around five minutes—I sliced some of the bread, put it and the butter on the table, and poured myself a timid glass of white wine. Checked the mussels. They were all opened up and smelling tomatoey and of the sea in an appetizing way. I was pleased at the appetizing part. I was beginning to feel like myself again.

Served the mussels in bowls; we mopped the sauce up with the bread, and then had a salad with blue cheese and lemon juice dressing in the bowls to mop up what the bread didn't get.

The wine felt lovely, to my delicate stomach's surprise. And my only regret was that I hadn't thought to add a slice of orange peel to the sauce—it would have been a nice flavor with the saffron and the Pernod and the thyme. And once I'm worrying about that kind of thing, well, I know I've left the stomach flu way behind.

There were more mussels at the market a few days later, looking bigger and hairier than the ones I bought before, but still appetizing, and by far the best deal and the freshest in the fish section. Also, Ken had just delivered my favorite sourdough bread to the store, so that it was still warm and quite irresistible. Also, I had exactly an hour from when I was due to get home to when I was due to go out again, so I needed something really quick and easy for dinner.

So it was mussels—again.

I thought about it all the way home, how to cook them this time, and I contemplated several different ways: with beer? with olive oil and garlic? with pesto from the freezer? But then the car did a slight, treacherous skid on the snowy road, and I remembered (I always need that first reminder every year) that it was winter and I had better slow down. So I thought about the easiest possible way I could cook them, and the most satisfying for a snowy winter's night.

This is what I did with them (for two people):

Put a little more than a pound of mussels in a bowl of salty water. This batch had beards on them (sometimes the fishmonger trims them off before packaging them; not this time, though), but I never take the beards off till right before cooking, since it kills the shellfish pretty fast. So I let them sit while I heated a little butter (about a tablespoon and a half) in the big enameled cast iron pot. I stewed a minced large shallot in the butter, and added a tablespoon of curry powder, too. Then I diced a Roma tomato and threw that in with a large glass of white wine. I let that cook down, salted it, added a little cream—just a slurp from the carton—and while that was heating, pulled the beards off the mussels. Then I put them in the pan in the midst of the bubbling sauce, clapped the lid on, and sliced some bread. Also toasted some pecans and crumbled some blue cheese into a bowl on top of them, with a couple of handfuls of mesclun lettuce. Set the table, put out the butter, poured myself a glass of wine, and the mussels were ready, all in about five minutes.

I sprinkled parsley on top of the mussels and spooned them into a couple of bowls. We ate them with the bread to mop up the sauce, and when we were finished, I tossed the greens and pecans and blue cheese first with a little olive oil and salt and pepper, and then with a tiny bit of sherry vinegar. We mopped up what was left in the bowls with the salad. And it was a very nice dinner indeed.

Mussels are great to eat around the holidays. They save you money, they save you time, they save you calories you can spend on Christmas chocolates instead, and they have a sort of festive atmosphere about them that's quite nice for the season.

And I even had time, before I went out, to salt some cod I'd bought for a Christmas Eve brandade de morue. That would take a little longer to cook, and it's a little more expensive, too, but satisfying in its own way. Very satisfying.

They grow these fabulous oysters on the Oregon coast, and we order them, of course, whenever we're lucky enough to be in a restaurant serving them up. I used to deeply regret that I couldn't get my hands on the same oysters myself.

But then one day, just out of the blue, my local Co-op started selling the very same oysters, shucked and nestled in their own juices. No hesitation when I saw them—I pounced. And had them that night, scalloped.

This is how:

For half a pint of oysters, which will feed two, make about a cup and a half of breadcrumbs. Sauté these in a couple of tablespoons of butter till golden. Mix breadcrumbs with minced parsley, minced garlic, minced scallions. (If you have a Cuisinart, first whirl the bread crumbs—crustless—then, while they're frying, whirl the parsley, garlic, and scallions.) Mix the parsley mixture with the cooled crumbs. Salt and pepper. Butter a shallow casserole dish—not very big, just enough to hold two layers of crumbs and one of oysters. Then layer half the crumbs, the oysters, sprinkle oysters with salt and pepper, layer the rest of the crumbs. Dribble cream on top, about two tablespoons. If you don't have cream, melt some more butter and dribble that. Bake in a 350° oven for about 25 minutes, till it looks golden and heavenly and smells of oysters. Serve with a salad made with a mustard vinaigrette in which you've marinated a sliced stalk of celery. White wine.

Heaven. And I didn't even have to leave the house.

For years now, the only canned tuna I've bought is one that caught my eye, one day, on the grocery shelf.

Its label was a plain white strip of paper with simple black lettering that said: "Fishing vessel Pisces Albacore. Product of USA. Contents: Albacore. Sea Salt." And on the back: "You are holding *North Pacific Albacore Tuna*, hook and line caught by the fishing vessel *Pisces*, then hand packed by a quality Oregon micro-cannery. Our albacore is filleted and canned with no additives except 15 grams of sea salt. This product is humanely harvested with no accidental capture of other species. Dolphins play at the bow while we fish!"

A hand drawn picture of a blue tuna holding a red heart was on the side.

It was, and is, at $4, an expensive can of tuna (although less now than when I first started buying it—now it seems a very reasonable price for almost half a pound of toxin free omega-3 fish). I started buying it because I was worried about mercury levels in most canned fish, and vaguely remembered that wild caught tuna from Pacific Northwest waters showed negligible levels of the stuff. Also, that sentence about the dolphins, with its final exclamation mark. Something about the whole label spoke to me of real people with a real job, working a small business their way.

Anyway, I bought it.

Once we'd tasted it, we never went back. There was no comparison between what came out of that can and Chicken of the Sea. Big meaty pieces of filet, with a hearty, honest taste to them. Everything I made with that tuna—and once I'd tasted it, I treated it with the respect it deserved—tasted like a party. Tuna and lentil salad with pita bread. Tuna sandwiches made with sourdough bread and aioli. Just the tuna by itself tossed with olive oil and lemon juice, on top of a bed of greens. It was all great. And it was all more than worth the money. From time to time, I wondered about that label, and about the people behind it. I wondered where they fished and how they fished, and, more importantly, why. Most of the time, though, I just enjoyed their tuna. I paid attention to it. It insisted, by its very integrity and taste that I pay attention to it. Which is what I want from my ingredients whenever I set out to make a meal.

Then, one day, I was shopping at my local Co-op, and passed a minor hubbub going on at the counter where they usually showcase products and give out samples. As I passed by, thinking about something else (goat cheese, as I recall, and whether Ken had arrived yet with the day's shipment of just baked bread), my eye was caught by a pyramid of the cans of what I by now thought of as My Tuna.

"Ah!" I said, skidding to a halt, "My Tuna! I've been buying that for years!"

Then I noticed her behind the cans. She was a little worried looking, and a little worn, but she had those sparkling eyes you read so much about. They sparkled now, and darted and shone. "That's MY tuna you've been buying," she said proudly. "And I'm so glad to meet you. I always wonder about our customers on the other end."

After assuring her enthusiastically that I had often wondered about her as well, and heartily praising her tuna, I finally got to ask: "Who made that label?"

"I did!" she said, and she laughed again. "I drew the fish! I was so proud of that fish! I'm glad you liked it!'

Then, as often happens, we settled down to talking. And she told me her story.

"When I was in school out on the coast, I started doing temp work going out on the fishing boats in the summer. Well, you know how it is. I fell in love with one of the guys, and we got married, and then we had our own boat. And we worked and worked and worked—you have no idea how hard we worked—but we just couldn't make it pay. Too much competition from the big boys. It was just too hard. So I finished my nursing degree, and we moved inland close to here. I liked it there, had a nice job, and he went into construction. Everything was fine, I thought.

"Then, I don't know what happened, whether it was a mid-life crisis, or what, but one day my husband just woke up and said, 'I'm sorry. I have to go back to fishing. That's what I have to do.' I thought to myself, well, this is just a phase he has to go through. He'll get over it. So I kept the house here and my job, and watched him move back to the coast and buy another boat. I'd commute out to keep him company—you know that drive's beautiful, but it's a long one. And after a couple of years, it dawned on me. This wasn't a mid-life crisis. And it wasn't going to go away.

"But I probably still would have stayed here, except that a friend of ours, a guy that fished from Alaska on down, who really knew what he was doing, went out one day alone in his boat and disappeared. They found parts of his boat floating later, but no one ever knew what had happened, whether there'd been some kind of explosion or what. And I said to my husband, 'Well, that's it. You're never going out on a boat alone again. I'm coming with you, and whatever happens to you will happen to me, too.' So I sold up the inland house and moved out and we went back to fishing."

Fortunately, this time the timing was right: shoppers were more aware of how hard the larger fleets were on the environment, on dolphins especially, and how the tuna packed by big business was frequently of inferior quality. This time, while it was still hard, they found they could make the fishing pay. But of course, if you've got a small business, you can't just fish. You've got to go out and sell your fish. And that's what she was doing today.

She gave me one of their pamphlets, with a picture of her standing, grinning widely, dressed in oilskin, holding up an enormous tuna. And I noticed there was no website, no email address, just phone numbers. I didn't ask her about that. I could just imagine, along with everything else they had to do, how impossible it would be to have a web presence as well. And somehow I found that a very comforting thought. The people who caught my tuna were too busy in the real world to worry much about the virtual.

We parted with warm expressions of esteem—and me with another couple of cans of tuna in my shopping cart. And I thought about her again the other night, during a heat wave, when I made a tuna niçoise pasta salad so good that my husband and I both sat there with our glasses of rosé just staring at it between bites. Not for long, though, since it was gone fast.

This was how, for two people for dinner, with a little left over that got doctored for a great lunch the next day:

In a colander in the sink, I put four diced Roma tomatoes, a half a sliced yellow onion, a chopped scallion, and a julienned jalapeno pepper. Tossed these with a tablespoon of coarse salt, covered with a plate and weighted it down to push out any bitter juices. I let those sit for a half an hour or so while . . .

In a big salad bowl, I put four halved anchovy fillets, a few chopped capers, about twelve pitted and torn Kalamata olives, a half a bunch of parsley minced, two quartered hard boiled eggs, and a can of Pisces tuna, broken into chunks. I squeezed a little lemon over this and tossed.

I put a pot on to cook a quarter pound of ziti pasta.

And made the salad dressing:

In a mortar, five cloves of garlic, the rest of the can of anchovies, some pepper, a little salt, the oil from the can of anchovies. I mashed all of this to a puree, then added red wine vinegar to taste.

Rinsed the salted vegetables in the colander and let them dry out a little while I cooked the pasta. Then added the vegetables to the salad bowl, drained the pasta in the colander, refreshed and cooled it with cold water. Shook the extra water off, then added it to the salad bowl with the rest of the ingredients, and the salad dressing.

Tossed very gently so as not to mash the eggs too much.

Served on a bed of spring greens, with lemon wedges on the side.

(*The next day, for the bit that was left, I added two grated carrots, another chopped scallion, some more minced parsley, some lemon juice and olive oil, and tossed the whole with a good amount of lettuce. We had that on top of whole wheat tortillas, topped with a little Greek yogurt, and a very good lunch it was, too.*)

There's really something different about cooking and eating food made by people you've met in circumstances you can understand. It makes you feel more closely knit into the social fabric, and it makes you feel less alone. And of course, by paying a little more, you're helping to reweave that social fabric, not just standing by helplessly watching it unravel. Not to mention how much better everything tastes when you sit down to dinner with your loved ones.

To order Pisces Tuna, contact Sally and Daryl Bogardus, PO

Box 812, Coos Bay, Oregon, 97420, USA. Phone numbers: (001) 541-266-7336, or the cell phone (001) 541-821-7117. *(They also have smoked albacore, Chinook salmon, smoked salmon, and various gift packs. I've tried the smoked albacore. It's really good with lentils, or mixed in a potato salad.)*

We had an anniversary coming up, and usually this means either a quiet trip to the beach with the dogs, or dinner at our favorite local restaurant. But this time, we both felt more like staying home. Too little cash, too little time, he'd been traveling too much to want to get in a car again . . . and I just went four hours away and four hours back with our young dog to rescue another dog from an animal shelter where she was unable to find a home. We wanted to stay with the dogs, too—the new dog was so tentatively thrilled to be here, safe and sound and among friends, who could bear to lock her up in a car while we ate inside?

So I wanted to make something festive for dinner, but not something that would involve a lot of fuss. Something that would let me settle down in front of the fire with my loved ones while it cooked. Normally, this would mean my version of paella. But I didn't really have the time or the money to race around looking for the best seafood and sausage to put into it. That left an arroz, my version of a Spanish rice dish, made with whatever bits and pieces I could find. Bits and pieces in Spanish is "pedacitos." So Arroz con Pedacitos. With aioli, to really dress it up and make it particularly nice.

The guys at my local Co-op fish counter know when they see

me coming that I'm going to scour the shelves for whatever they've got of fish scraps, packaged and sold cheap. I buy them when I see them, and toss 'em in the freezer against just such a need as this one. So I had a couple of packages of halibut frames, with a good amount of fish still clinging to the nicely gelatinous bones—$1.99 a pound. And I had a yogurt container full of fish stock in the freezer, made the last time I put together an arroz.

Fish stock—any kind of stock—is easy if you don't worry yourself too much about it. Just throw what non oily fish scraps and bones, along with shrimp shells (when you eat shrimp, don't throw out the shells left on the plate, decant them into a plastic bag and freeze them for making stock later), in a saucepan along with a cleaned carrot (or peelings), a stick of celery (or peelings—if you have them), a bit of onion or top of a leek, an unpeeled garlic clove or two, a bay leaf, some peppercorns, and sprigs of parsley and/or thyme.

Don't worry if you don't have some of this, or if you have other things instead that might make it taste nice—fennel fronds, say, or chard ribs, or a little bit of lemon peel. Just imagine what the combination would taste like and add, then cover with water. Bring to a boil. Simmer for about a half an hour, then take out the fish skeletons and shred what fish there is on the bones into a bowl. Set aside. Put the bones back in the stock and simmer some more, until the liquid tastes nice. At this point, you can freeze it, or keep it simmering to add to the arroz.

Of course if you have it in the freezer already—and luckily, this time, I did—the dish is a breeze. I just heated up the stock, added the fish skeletons, cooked till the fish on them shredded, took them out, saving the fish—and that was my nicely deepened stock. While that was cooking, I made the aioli. If you make it in the food processor or the blender—one whole fresh egg whipped with some salt, one cup of ½ olive oil, ½ sunflower oil added SLOWLY, then mixed with at least five pureed garlic cloves and a little lemon juice—it takes hardly any time at all. And it's so delicious, it makes us scrape the plate with our fingers to get the last bit up. We can do this when it's just the two of us, which is one reason why eating at home is so delightful. That, and that we can eat in our bathrobes if we feel like it.

Now the arroz. For two, with leftovers for next day's lunch:

Get a wide pot or skillet out, one with a good fitting lid. Pour in a little olive oil—Spanish is nicest for this. Heat gently, and sauté a chopped onion until it's soft. Add a few chopped cloves of garlic (or just one, if you're not as crazy about garlic as we are) and a minced hot pepper. Cook for awhile on the lowest heat till everything's soft but not browned, almost melting together. Salt. Then add a teaspoon and a half of pimenton de vera—Spanish smoked paprika. Stir so it doesn't scorch. Add a diced tomato or two, and continue cooking on a low heat until the whole thing is like savory jam.

While this is going on, soak a couple of pinches of saffron in a little bit of wine. (I also use this time to make a salad dressing for our first course, and to set the table.)

Now. Add 1½ cups short grain BROWN RICE. Really. Please try it. It tastes divine, really meaty and much more interesting than that upper class white stuff you've been using. Yes, I know it takes longer, but so what? That's just more time to sit with your loved one and a glass of wine, isn't it? And this is a festival after all.

Stir the rice until it crackles. Now add 4 cups of simmering fish stock. Maybe a little more salt at this point—taste. Bring back to a boil, add the wine and saffron, clap the lid on, turn the heat onto the lowest setting, and set the timer for an hour. (You'll have to check from time to time till you get used to the heat of your own burners. If it's boiling too quickly, even on the lowest heat, use a flame tamer. That's what I do, but my burners burn hot. On the other hand, if the rice isn't tender in an hour, and there's still liquid, take the lid off, turn the heat up a bit, and watch it till it's near done, then clap the lid back on, turn the heat down, and let it go another five minutes.)

Use the hour to pour yourself and loved one a glass of something, and sit down with a few olives to nibble on. I had a bottle of inexpensive Spanish Rosé Cava all ready to go, and go it did.

We had a glass or two of that, and a pre-prandial wander 'round the meadow in the dusk with the dogs, and when the timer went off, I had a look at how the rice was doing. When it was nearly done, I added the reserved fish bits, and some frozen peas straight from the package for color . . . maybe a drained jar of artichoke hearts I had sitting in the cupboard . . . then I let it cook another few minutes until it smelled wonderful. We sat down to a salad while I let the arroz rest a little off the heat. Then out it came, spooned in a beautiful bronzed pool onto white plates with a dollop of aioli and lemon wedges on the side. More aioli on the table. And more Cava of course.

That's my idea of a fiesta. Really. (Oh, and for dessert, slices of quince paste, if you can find it, alternating with slices of Monterey Jack cheese. Eat a bit of both in one bite. It sounds weird, but it's completely creamy and delicious, and the whole is more than the parts . . . which, come to think of it, was what we were celebrating on our anniversary, too.)

We used to have paella for Christmas. I liked the thought that octopus was a traditional holiday ingredient in our house. And I have spent many years perfecting a paella made with brown rice. We'd have it with a blue cheese and walnut dressed salad beforehand, and lots of red wine. Delicious.

Until a few years ago, when I realized it was silly to buy fresh seafood on Christmas Eve and keep it overnight just for some kind of formal celebration. I mean, when you have fresh seafood, you should eat it. That's one of the few rules I live by, or should, anyway. So we shifted, and now have our paella the night before.

This left me with a dilemma. How to make another quasi-vegetarian celebratory meal on the day itself. So we've had stuffed Portobello mushrooms. We've had oyster stew (really good that). We've had a lavish cheese platter.

This year, during a bout of pre-Christmas insomnia, which I spent, as usual, poring over my cookbook collection, I suddenly thought: "Brandade. Brandade. Definitely Brandade."

Brandade being mashed potatoes if mashed potatoes had gone first to sea and then to heaven . . . being mashed potatoes and mashed salt cod mashed with cream and olive oil and lots and lots of garlic. (I try to eat it whenever I'm in Paris. I've discovered a couple of nice little restaurants that way, by noticing it marked on a blackboard as the special of the day—salt cod on the menu being, as I think, a sign of serious culinary intent.)

But where to get the salt cod? We don't live, let me tell you, near a salt cod kind of a town. No Portuguese or Italian delis for miles. But then I had one of those moments where you suddenly realize you've been roaming the world for the Pearl of Great Price, and all the time it was sitting on your desk, forgotten, used as a paperweight. We get a lot of Alaskan cod here this time of year, and I always ignore it. Not anymore. Salting cod, it turns out, is easy. Why I never did it before I'm sure I can't think.

So this is what I did:

A few days before Christmas (salt cod keeps for ten days, if you keep salting it), I bought a little more than a pound of cod. I got a glass pan big enough to lay it out flat in, and sprinkled about a quarter cup of coarse salt on the bottom, laid the cod on top, and sprinkled another quarter cup of salt on top. Covered it with plastic wrap, popped it in the fridge. Every twelve hours, I just poured off whatever liquid accumulated and sprinkled a little more salt on.

Twenty-four hours before I wanted to cook it, I rinsed the cod and laid it in fresh water, which I changed two or three times. That was it—salt cod. So then I was ready for my brandade.

I checked every recipe I had in the house—you'd be surprised how many brandade recipes it turns out you probably have lurking about—and noticed that every one said their way was the only one. But every way was a different one. Now what that says to me is that the dish is pretty much indestructible, so I was pretty confident that

I could set about doing it my way, unharmed.

And indeed, so it was.

Let me say that brandade, made with less oil and cream than your general recipe recommends, baked till it browns on top or until you feel like eating it, whichever comes first, turns out to be an absolutely celestial, celebratory, irresistible dish of the kind that you can convince yourself your imaginary French great aunt used to make.

So this is how:

Put one pound desalted salt cod cut in big pieces into a large pot, big enough to hold it all in one layer. If you have them about, put carrot and celery trimmings, a bay leaf, a garlic clove, and a sprig of thyme in with the cod. (Don't fuss if you don't. I happened to be making crudités to go with our first course, so just threw the peelings in as I went. It would have been even better if I'd simmered the water with the peelings first, then let it cool, THEN added the cod. But it was just fine the way it was.) Bring slowly to a low simmer, just to where bubbles start to show a boil. Clap on a lid and let it sit for fifteen minutes.

Meanwhile, peel a large potato, quarter it, cover it with water and simmer for fifteen minutes or until tender when pierced by a fork. Peel some garlic cloves. Two if you are a moderate garlic eater, or, if you're like us, six. I highly recommend six.

Also, have a third of a cup of olive oil sitting on the stove in a Pyrex cup. And about three tablespoons of cream in another one. The point of this is to warm them, taking the chill off, so they'll mix better later. Most recipes say to warm them in separate pans, but I find it's easier just to put them near warm places. You don't want them hot, just tepid.

When the cod is done, scoop it out and lay it on a plate till it's cool enough to handle, and you can feel it to get out any little bones that might still be lurking. Get them all out.

Now put the garlic cloves and some pepper into a Cuisinart or blender. Get them nice and pureed. Add the salt cod and the drained cooked potato. Blend to as smooth or chunky as you like, or, if you're using a food processor, pulse to mash. Add the oil and cream in a stream while you pulse.

The brandade should look like mashed potatoes.

Taste. Heavenly, eh?

Now you have some choices. You can serve as is with crudités as a dip. You can decant into a warm bowl, surround with garlic rubbed toasts, and serve as a first course. Or, you can do what I did . . . which I am now sure is the very best thing to do.

Decant the brandade into a nice heatproof bowl. When you're ready, drizzle some more cream on top and put it into a 350° oven for about twenty minutes or so. If you like, you can stick it under the broiler for a minute to get it good and browned.

For some reason, putting it into the oven made my brandade puff up like a cloud. We had our first course by the fire, with champagne, while it cooked, and then came to table to have the brandade itself with a salad, some garlic rubbed toast, and more champagne.

This was about as festive a dinner as it gets. And now, our traditional Christmas foods are not just boring old octopus and squid. Not anymore.

Turnips and Squash

This is the Single Most Delicious Thing to do with Turnip Greens.

Now, I know you're saying: There ARE no delicious things to do with turnip greens. But you are wrong. Trust me. Dead wrong.

There are many delicious things to do with turnip greens: Cook them with bacon and garlic. With olive oil and lemon. With smoked paprika and ham.

BUT THE MOST DELICIOUS THING OF ALL TO DO WITH TURNIP GREENS IS AS FOLLOWS:

I discovered this wholly by accident. It was a really hot day, and I planned on cold noodles with a Japanese dipping sauce for dinner. But what vegetable? There were LOTS of turnips in the garden. So I made a grated turnip salad, and then I had all these greens. And there, in Elizabeth Andoh's *Japanese Cooking,* was a recipe for spinach with sesame seeds. Nothing to lose, I figured. I replaced the spinach with the turnip greens. It was transcendent. Really, truly. And simple. The only odd thing you need for this dish—and you really do need it—is a Japanese suribachi, which is a grooved mortar with a pestle. There's just no other way to mash the sesame seeds to a paste.

This is how you do it for two people:

¾ to 1 lb. of turnip greens. I just eye-balled my batch; you don't need to be too precise. This will look like a lot of greens, but will cook down to practically nothing by the time you're through. No yellow or tough leaves, get rid of the stems. Bring big pot of water to boil, salt it, add the turnip greens. Cook till tender. Drain and immediately rinse with cold water to stop cooking. When cool enough to handle, squeeze out every bit of water you can from the greens. Chop.

Three tablespoons of sesame seeds. Roast at 300° until toasty—watch carefully, it takes about five minutes, but then they blacken fast. They'll smell sesame-ish when done.

Put them in the suribachi and mash them until pasty. Add 1 tablespoon of sugar, keep mashing till pastier. Slowly add 2 and a half tablespoons of soy sauce.

Add the chopped greens to the sauce (just add them to the suribachi; that's easiest). Toss. Chill.

Serve. Watch as your loved one gets a kind of "oh, well, greens are good for me" look on his face, and then watch that look turn slowly to pure delight as the taste sinks in.

(For lunch the next day, I tried it with chicory, which I couldn't even remember why I asked for it to be planted. I held my breath, sure I was pushing my luck, and discovered that sesame seeds mashed with soy sauce and sugar make any greens taste like a Japanese dream. But it was the turnip greens that tasted best of all.)

Then there's a turnip omelet . . . which, when the turnips are young and sweet, is one of the most delicious things you will ever taste.

For two people:

Grate about a pound of peeled turnips. Salt and leave in a colander for about twenty minutes, then squeeze out any bitter juice.

Toss the grated turnip in a quarter cup of butter on medium heat until tender. Add a little chopped herb. I used marjoram; Richard Olney (whose recipe this is) specifies savory. Thyme would be good, too. Add a quarter cup chopped parsley.

Then, for two people, blend five eggs. (I used four eggs and an egg white, because I used the fifth yellow for a mayonnaise. That worked splendidly.) Mix with cooled turnip mixture, salt and pepper, and then cook as you would your favorite frittata. If you don't have a favorite way, here's how I do it:

Heat a tablespoon of butter in a skillet (nonstick is easiest, I'm afraid to say). When hot enough to make a drop of water sizzle, pour in the egg/turnip mixture, spread it around in the pan. Lift edges up, let egg slide around and fill up spaces. Cook on medium heat until bottom is browned. Meanwhile, heat up broiler. Stick under low heat broiler for a minute or two, until the top is cooked. Not too cooked, mind.

When done, turn over onto a dish, so the brown side is up. Serve warm or room temperature.

Now, what I did with that extra yolk . . . I made an aioli, which, as you already know, is a mayonnaise with crushed garlic. Lots of crushed garlic. I cooked a cup of chickpeas, and when they were done, tossed them with the aioli and lots and lots of chopped parsley. We had this with the turnip omelet.

A green salad to start.

Alex murmured all the way through, the way he does when I know I've made a hit. And then he said: that was one of my favorite dinners ever.

Of course, he was the one who grew the turnips. But still.

Then there's the squash issue. It comes up every year. The zucchini/yellow squash population explosion, both in the garden and at the store. The stuff's so fresh, and cheap, I want to use it everywhere, but there's so much of it. I have to admit it, there are times when the beautiful emerald and yellow piles make me feel helpless. Hopeless. Like I can't effect change.

But there is something I can do. I can take direct action, and yet enjoy the zucchini/squash crop to the utmost . . . and I can do it without making zucchini bread!

As my husband's yellow crookneck squash plants throw out the ominous dozens of fruits that form at the ends of the dozens of vines, I make up my mind to conquer rather than be conquered.

For example. Let me tell you what we had for dinner one of those nights in squash season:

Crookneck squash with mushrooms and chipotle chile.

Avocado, tomato, chile, scallion, and cilantro salad w/lime.

Garlic-infused brown rice.

Shredded Monterey Jack cheese.

Heated corn tortillas.

This is a lovely dinner. The garlic rice is from a Diana Kennedy recipe (you just whirl garlic cloves and a bit of green pepper in the food processor with a little water, and add that first to the rice, before adding the rest of the water and settling it to cook). The Avocado etc. salad is my chunky version of guacamole, which, due to our tastes, generally ends up as a cilantro salad flavored with the other ingredients. The shredded Jack cheese needs no other description.

The squash dish is fabulous (this for two people with enough left over to make tacos for next day's lunch). *(Feel free to use zucchini, yellow squash, crookneck squash, pattypan squash . . . etc. I know I would.)*

I finely minced a half red onion and added 2 minced chipotle chilies with it to a wide skillet heating a bit of sunflower oil. Cooked this on low heat just to wilt. Meanwhile, I diced about 6 or 7 squash, and when the onion was cooked but not browned, I added them to the skillet with some salt. Coated them with the oil, then covered and turned the heat to low. I cooked for ten minutes, till squash was tender.

In another skillet (this is a Diana Kennedy idea, and it does make a difference to the taste), over medium high heat, I tossed about a ¼ pound cremini mushrooms, quartered, in a little oil and salt, until they were browned and mushroomy, about five minutes. I did this while the squash were cooking and the tortillas heating in the toaster oven.

Then I tossed the mushrooms with the squash. You can cover it all with chopped cilantro now, if you like—if you don't think that's too much cilantro for one meal. Definitely cover it with shredded cheese, reserving some for the table. Then cover and turn off the heat while you get everyone to sit down.

Once the cheese has melted, serve.

This looks nice on the plate: a crescent of brown rice. On one side overlapping the rice, a helping of squash. Overlapping the other side, a helping of guacamole.

Serve with the tortillas, reserved shredded cheese, and hot sauce.

Also—if you're so inclined—BEER.

And for one day, that harvest of squash is beautifully under control.

Three new big squashes. Better pick them before they become watery monsters. What to do? As usually happens in periods of garden anxiety, a quick look at Richard Olney's *Simple French Food* saves the day. Reading it, one has the impression that Olney spent all of his time mulling over the most individual and creative ways to deal with the market, the garden, the kitchen, the table. He's persnickety, but my, the persnickety-ness comes with the attention that only accompanies True Love.

Anyway, he had three recipes for zucchini gratin. I slightly adapted the third for our crookneck squash . . . easy, and so delicious I used it again another night with the yellow squash.

This was how:

1 lb. squash (yellow, zucchini, etc.) sliced thin. (Olney uses a

mandoline; I, hearty West Coast lug that I am, don't bother).

Toss over high heat in a little olive oil till slightly browned and limp.

Oil a shallow gratin dish.

Soak about 2 ounces stale, crustless bread in hot water, drain, and squeeze out as much liquid as you can.

Dice about 3 ounces Swiss cheese . . . small dice is good because it melts in better.

Mash two cloves of garlic in a mortar. Chop lots of parsley. Mix with the garlic.

In a bowl, mix 1 egg with the bread, the garlic and parsley, the cheese, salt and pepper. When the squash is cool, add that.

Spread into gratin dish, smooth out, dribble a little oil on top.

Bake in top third of 425° oven for half an hour.

We had this with sautéed potatoes and peas from the garden.

Sometime I'm going to try the same dish, but with whole wheat bread. Then again, I might add a little rice. Maybe Parmesan instead of Swiss cheese? And then, there's so much basil, maybe instead of the parsley . . . or better with the parsley . . . or . . .

There'll be plenty of chances to experiment. There's a lot more squash to come.

In squash season, it's not just Alex's garden I have to deal with. I have The Indigo Ray's squash plants, too. And whenever I go over to her five acres of organic garden, I come home with bags and bags of the stuff. And not just squash stuff, either.

The other night, I was looking at what I'd so casually picked in her garden: a huge heap of green beans, a monster orange tomato, herbs, and a couple of zucchini.

So this is what we had for dinner:

Warm salad with curly endive and walnuts. (I shredded the endive; I like that better with a warm salad of bitter leaves.)
A tomato clafouti.
Green beans tossed in pesto.
Zucchini tian, adapted from a Deborah Madison cookbook.

The zucchini tian (to continue an utterly squash themed summer) was the most memorable item.

Slice an onion and two garlic cloves. Chop a handful of whatever herb you have around (I used, at Deborah Madison's advice, a combo of thyme, rosemary, and sage.) Sauté onion and garlic and half the herbs with a little oil until translucent. Or browned. Or whatever you like, as long as not blackened.

Spread these on the bottom of a gratin dish.

Slice the zucchini thinly. In the same pan, toss with a little oil and the rest of the herbs, until starting to brown (about ten minutes).

Put this on top of the onions.

Then slice whatever spare cherry tomatoes you have around, or Romas, or whatever. (I used some green cherry tomatoes that fell early, along with a couple of orange ones for color.)

Tuck these and some torn up, pitted olives in with everything else.

Bake at 375° for ½ hour.

It's great warm or at room temperature. And Alex got the rest of it for his lunch the next day, with toast and ricotta salata, while I ran some errands in town.

And finally, a small but significant victory over squash—for one person:

An eight inch yellow squash or zucchini or gnarled crookneck squash, sliced, diced, or dealt with in whatever way you like.

One garlic clove, minced.

Some fresh mint, minced, about a tablespoon.

A half a large tomato, diced.

Warm some olive oil in a sauté pan. When it's hot, turn heat up to high, and throw in the squash (or zucchini or etc.). Toss for a moment until it starts to brown. Throw in the minced garlic and mint, turn the heat down, add the tomato. Cook for a few minutes on medium low, until tomato mushes into the squash, and the squash is tender. Salt and pepper. Serve.

This is particularly good with bacon and creamy fried eggs served atop sourdough toast . . . for a solitary supper.

It would have been delicious at room temperature, too, as a salad with a lemon wedge on the plate, but I didn't wait that long to find out.

It's Just Not a Meal
Without Potatoes

(Once, long ago, in a galaxy far, far away, I lived smack dab in the middle of an area famous for its potatoes. And every day, on the radio, an announcer would say: "The Malin Chamber of Commerce would like to remind you that . . . it's just not a meal without . . . potatoes." Which was really a very nice way to put it . . .)

Potato salad is a perfect example of what we might call Recipe Fear of Failure. You know what I mean. The cookbooks that come out relentlessly every year change their minds about what you must and must not do about such a wide variety of things that I often wonder just how in God's name we all stand it. Do we really need someone to tell us that we MUST use waxy potatoes for a perfect effect?

Apparently so.

It's interesting to watch the evolution of this kind of thing. When I was in my twenties, these recipes used to terrify me. Waxy potatoes? Oh my Lord. I don't even know what a WAXY POTATO is. Somehow I had this feeling that if I didn't use waxy potatoes, something would explode. Or the person I served the salad to would stop loving me and instantly leave me for the snide girl with big breasts who my mother thought was so much funnier than I was. Or I would be a failure in . . . in what? Whatever.

Here is a great pleasure about getting older, and it's a pleasure I want to freely share with anyone who needs or would like it: you get to watch these recipes change, you get to watch the stern mothers and dads of the cooking world go 180 degree turns, while insisting, the whole trip, that this point on the compass—no, THIS one—is the real, true, only way.

Diana Kennedy (who by the way, is in my top ten pantheon of writers, let alone cookbook writers) is a hilarious example of this. Read her early cookbooks. They are models of culinary dogmatism. You must use a special kind of Saran wrap because, apparently, some Mexican confidante of hers did. By her latest books, though, she's been thoroughly beaten up by life—lucky for us. And her attitude now is, "What the hell. Whatever tastes good. Who cares if it was originally made by Spanish nuns in a convent outside of Durango?"

But she, come to think of it, is an example of a passionately sincere writer who believes deeply in what she writes. She didn't do a 180 degree turn so much as evolve. Writers like Kennedy—those kind of people—have a lot to say.

The ones you want to look out for, and I mean to the extent of putting a metaphoric dagger through their black hearts and burying them under a full moon in a lead coffin, are the careerists. The careerist food writers. You can easily tell these guys. Whatever is the latest thing, they're for it. They all know where El Bulli is and who Thomas Keller trained (according to the cooking magazines, as far as I can tell, that's every publicized chef in the known world). They're for balsamic vinegar the minute everyone else is; they act like they're the first people in the world to drink whatever wines are suddenly all over the mass media (when this happens, suspect a new media consultant hired on by whatever product you're seeing pop up). I loathe them. Or perhaps not them—their works. I have sympathy for them, mind you. It's not easy making a living by carefully plotting a slight superiority to an audience that can turn on you in a second—kind of like working as a shark trainer when you have a bad paper cut on your hand. But the incredible stance that they know more than you do, and that they have to maintain that superiority in order to keep the whole machine turning over . . . I get so I want to overthrow our entire economic system just to set them and us free.

But you and I don't have to wait for the revolution to claim our own autonomy. We can make potato salad with whatever the hell we have in the kitchen. And the only thing that matters is that we enjoy it and our loved ones enjoy it too.

Back in the days when I couldn't figure out what a waxy potato was, I used russets or Idahos (I think they're the same; they look the same to me, anyway). I loved the way they crumbled and mushed bits of themselves into the salads. I felt guilty about this, mind, because every new cookbook I had said that THE IMPORTANT THING ABOUT POTATO SALAD WAS THE INTEGRITY OF THE POTATOES. My potatoes, I had to sadly admit, were a complete failure in the integrity department. They didn't hold together, let alone hold their own. Instead, they joined with the rest of the ingredients to make a kind of celestial tasting hash.

Of course, I eventually figured out the waxy potato thing. Red potatoes, Yukon gold potatoes, boiling potatoes: they're bung full of that kind of integrity. But I didn't mess with them until recently, when the cooking mags and cookbooks began to stertorously announce that you MUST USE RUSSET POTATOES for potato salad, or be cast out into the darkness. It turns out that now that crumbling and mushing thing I was so embarrassed to love is just what you need for a new, hip, fresh, retro look at potato salad. Waxy potatoes . . . well. They're so . . . yesterday.

So now I felt sorry for those poor red potatoes. Perversely, when these new recipes appeared, dogmatically agreeing with what I had secretly thought all along, I started buying the waxy ones instead.

And you know what? It doesn't matter what kind of potato you use for potato salad. It doesn't matter what kind of onion, either. It turns out they're all great.

What you need for potato salad:

Enough potatoes for the amount of people you want to feed. You cut these in the shape you feel like. I like diced or sliced, myself.

Then you cook them whatever way you feel like. You can boil them. You can bake them whole and cut them later. I like to steam them after they're cut up. So I do.

Then you put them in a big bowl and while they're still hot sprinkle them with some white wine, or lemon juice, or a little light vinegar. Even some chicken broth. They'll soak this up and be tastier.

Now you add chopped onion of any kind (chives, white mild onion, red onion, scallions, shallots, onion tops from the plants you have in the garden) . . . and/or minced garlic . . . and as much chopped herbs as you like. Parsley for sure. Then one other, a mild one, if you have it: dill, or basil, or chervil. Tarragon, or marjoram, is good, too, but you need to use a lighter hand with these. The other three you can just chop and add at will.

Toss with the dressing of your choice. A plain vinaigrette. A mustard vinaigrette. Mayonnaise. Garlic mayonnaise. Sour cream. Yogurt. A mix of mayo and sour cream. Or mayo and yogurt. Or yogurt and mustard if you're dieting. I like garlic mayonnaise.

Salt and pepper, of course.

Serve hot, warm, or cold. On a bed of shredded lettuce is nice.

This is what I did the other night:

Diced red potatoes, steamed, then sprinkled with white wine. I added chopped onion tops from the onion plants in the garden, and almost a whole chopped bunch of parsley. Lots of dill. Alex had harvested some really sweet peas, so I shelled those and added them raw. I had a bowl of Garlic Mayonnaise (aka aioli) in the fridge, so tossed the salad with a few spoonfuls of that, salted and peppered, and served immediately, still warm, with sandwiches: bacon, lettuce, avocado, tomato and aioli for me, and extra sharp Cheddar, lettuce, avocado, tomato and aioli for him. Glass of rosé for me, a local ale for him. Unbelievably delicious and perfect for the three digit heat.

And don't get me started on Salade Niçoise . . .

On a cold and clear night, my thoughts turned again to vegetable stew for dinner . . . and a wilted celery salad with a mustard vinaigrette. That one I like to make with dumplings.

Now that vegetable stew is always an improvisation based on

how I'm feeling at the moment . . . so this particular night found me putting down a base of finely minced onions, carrot, celery, mushroom stems, garlic stewed in oil and butter, then adding some tomato paste and herbs (parsley, sage, rosemary, and thyme—yes, that's right), then red wine, then chopped tomatoes, then big chunks of what I had on hand . . . a couple of purple potatoes, a half a red onion, three cut up carrots, a couple of pieces of celery, a lot of chunked mushrooms, some baby yellow squash saved from the last frost, whole garlic cloves, more thyme, a bay leaf, a lovage leaf . . . and at the last minute, I couldn't resist it, a bit of organic orange peel and a slug of Pernod from the cupboard. Covered the whole thing with water and then salt. Simmered till veggies were done. The gravy was a little too thin for my liking, so I poured the liquid into another pan and boiled it down till it tasted great, then thickened it with a beurre manié—about a tablespoon of butter mashed with a tablespoon of flour, then whisked into the sauce.

I put the sauce back in with the veggies. At this point, I added some frozen spinach and frozen peas for a splash of green color. Heated it all through till nice and melded. Corrected the seasoning.

But what about dumplings? We usually have dumplings with this, and the Beloved Husband was expecting them. But I just didn't think, when I tasted things on my mind's palate, that dumplings GO with Pernod and orange peel.

So this is the recipe I wanted to share here. I already had it in the refrigerator.

I don't know what to call this. "Potatoes cooked earlier and then smooshed with what sour cream or cream and/or butter is available, along with mashed garlic and pepper and chopped parsley and then smoothed in a baking dish, and then covered with either little bits of butter or dribbled with cream, or both, and then topped with shredded cheese (I used Parmesan this particular night, but Swiss is good, Jack is great, Cheddar superb, and so on) and sprinkled with paprika. Then baked for twenty minutes or so at 350° till nice and brown and crusty."

That's the best title I can give it, I suppose.

The point of this potato dish is that you make it on a night you're baking potatoes for dinner. Just add a half dozen more than you think you'll need, and decant the baked insides into a baking dish with the cream, garlic, pepper, parsley, etc. Stick into the fridge for when you might need it.

I needed it just then with the veggie stew. I baked it as above, then served squares of it in a bowl, napped by the stew. Celery salad in little bowls. Red wine. Chocolate and dried fruit for dessert.

A perfect fall dinner. The B.H. never missed the dumplings. And he had thirds.

Potatoes and Chilies is is one of those dishes that sound absolutely bizarre, but then when you taste it, your inner child coos with delight. The first time I had it was in a Chinese Muslim restaurant whose name I refuse to reveal—there's already too long a wait for a table—and I only ordered it because my dining companion and I are both part Irish, and it cracked us up to think of Irish and

Chinese food on the same plate.

It was heavenly. I never forgot it. I never saw it again either, until . . . until . . . well, I have to thoroughly recommend Mark Bittman's cookbook, *The Best Recipes in the World*. (The title's no lie. I have, up till now, cooked from this cookbook the best asparagus and fried eggs, the best quick pickled cucumbers and zucchini, the best steamed fish, the best sesame noodles . . . I could go on.) There it was, surprising me in the middle of his cookbook. "Potatoes and Chilies." And since the Beloved Husband's ur-food is potatoes, and since his affection for chile plants leads him every year to overstock the garden with more Scoville units than any normal family can use comfortably, it seemed a natural—if only to get rid of some of those chilies.

He'd been growing a Peruvian yellow chile called an aji, and he absolutely fawned on those plants. Responding to his great love, the plants produced madly. Hotly and madly. They're a really fruity chile, delicious, but you can't eat a whole bunch of them at once. At least, I thought you couldn't, but it turns out that with the potatoes you can. You get their flavor and not so much of their heat.

Here's how you do it (I've adapted the Bittman recipe, predictably, to make it a little less mild).

Bring a big pot of water to the boil. While that's happening, peel and grate 4 or so potatoes (I used 6 medium-ish ones—Yukon Golds because that was what the Chinese/Muslim cooks used, and let me tell you, that was the right choice. But use what you have or what you like, as always.) When the water boils, salt, add the potatoes and blanch for thirty seconds . . . not so they're cooked, just so they're tender crisp. Drain.

Julienne 4 aji chilies. (Bittman recommends two minced Thai chilies, or 1 jalapeno, or 5 to 10 small dried chilies. In the Chinese/ Muslim restaurant, they julienned yellow chile and lots of it, so I tried to recreate that.) Put a couple of tablespoons of peanut or neutral oil (I used sunflower) in a skillet over medium high heat. Add the chilies, cook till they sizzle. Add the potatoes, cook, stirring all the time, till they brown, about 5 minutes. Salt and pepper. Taste. Adjust seasoning.

Eat right away. You'll be glad you did.

We had these with corn on the cob and Bittman's pickled cucumbers, and the inner children around here were in a good mood that night. In fact, the inner children said I could have used even more chilies, which was a good thing to know.

A Potato-Onion-Arugula-Rosemary frittata is always good. I love frittatas. I love them hot, I love them room temperature, I love them cold. You can put just about anything into them, or nothing but a few herbs, and change them around like those easy to accessorize black dresses that "go everywhere from day to night." Pretty much the basic pattern is this: stew some vegetables in butter or oil till cooked. Cool and mix with stirred eggs. Add chopped parsley, or mashed garlic, or bits of cheese, or any combination of the above. Salt and pepper. Heat oil in a skillet (only use butter if you're going to eat the frittata hot . . . butter isn't as good as it should be when it re-congeals). Pour in the egg mixture, lift it and swirl it like you do a regular omelet. Turn the heat down and let it cook for awhile till it looks fairly done on the bottom and is a nice brown there. Then either 1.) flip it over (I never do this without it ending in tears, but you're probably more adept than me), or 2.) put in a 400° oven till it cooks through, or 3.) (my preferred option) stick it under the broiler till it's done the way you like it and a little browned on top. Watch it carefully if you do this; you don't want it turning to leather.

One night it happened that we didn't have any bread, so I decided on a potato frittata. There was a lot of arugula about to bolt in the garden, so I whacked off a good three or four handfuls of that. And I had a brief yen for rosemary, which I don't usually in the summer, but there it was. So I cut a little branch with some nice juicy needles on it.

So this is what I did.

Heated some oil in a nonstick skillet. Added two peeled, thinly sliced Russet potatoes and half an onion diced. Salt. Cooked gently with a lid on until the potatoes were done but nothing was browned. Chopped my handfuls of arugula, threw them in, stirred around till they wilted, then took the whole thing off the heat to cool.

Meantime, stirred five eggs in a bowl, added some mashed garlic, salt and pepper, and the rosemary leaves chopped.

When the vegetables were cool, I poured them into the eggs, gave a stir, wiped out the skillet with a paper towel, put it back on a medium flame to heat with a little oil. (I also, at this point, turned the broiler on to heat.) When hot enough to make a flick of water off my fingers sizzle, I poured in the eggs. Swirled them around, lifted them up to let the eggs firm up and make a good base. Turned the heat down to low and cooked for a few more minutes, till I could see the bottom was done through the still liquid top.

Then I stuck the pan under the broiler unit for about two or three minutes till the top was done the way I like it. (Make sure if you do this that your skillet is ovenproof. I've forgotten before, and what it did to the plastic handle and the smell in my kitchen was ugly.) Pulled it out and left it to cool till dinner.

This would serve three people with a lot of other accompaniments, or two people, maybe with some left over for lunch. It would probably only serve one and a half teenagers, but odds are if you are a teenager or you feed one, I didn't have to tell you that.

We had cold boiled artichokes to start, dipped in a garlic mayonnaise made earlier in the day. Then we had the frittata. As a salad on the side, asparagus also boiled earlier, and then left out to cool spritzed with lemon (you can sprinkle olive oil on, too—I didn't bother because I knew we'd slather them with more mayonnaise). At room temperature, they're so suave, those fresh asparagus.

(As for the leftovers: the day after, for lunch, I mixed some hot chickpeas with the leftover garlic mayonnaise and served them over shredded lettuce and grated carrot, with the leftover frittata diced on top. We used warmed whole wheat pita bread to scoop the whole lot up. Hot sauce added at will.)

Eggs and Mushrooms

I love eggs. Not just any kind of eggs, mind. The kind of eggs that come from happy chickens. Eggs with real yellow yolks that show the chicken's been scouring the yard for something good for a chicken to eat. Eggs where the yolk sits up when you break it, instead of spreading out kind of depressed all over the plate. Real eggs. Not those crap eggs you get from torture chickens for about $1.50 a dozen, which make you think bleakly, for some reason, of World War II.

So when the foxes got all of Dawn the Egg Lady's chickens last year, we practically went into mourning around the house. I mean there was no replacing the eggs that come from Dawn's chickens. Those chickens lived in a cozy henhouse attached to the back of the house, they spread out during the day all over the garden, apparently unafraid of the three black Lab dogs they shared it with. They ate scraps. And their eggs were the kind of eggs you dream about if you are given, as I am, to dreaming about eggs.

The last year has been a makeshift one, with us bravely trying various types of Chino free range and organic eggs (fine, expensive, and not particularly an egg to make you immediately think of eggs for dinner), and local eggs on sale at the Co-op. I always try to get local eggs before they disappear into someone else's shopping cart (they go fast around here, those local eggs), but even when I do get them, I can tell a big difference between them and the Eggs of Dawn the Egg Lady. The only thing I can figure is the chickens that laid them must all get fed corn. There's a kind of pallid uniformity to the taste that makes me suspect those chickens rarely see a potato peel or a stray cantaloupe seed. The yolks aren't nearly as rich as the ones in Dawn's eggs, and they don't make the Beloved Vegetarian Husband give a contented sigh when he eats them, either. He likes them, all right, but I don't get the aural cues I'm waiting for.

When Dawn told me her new chicks were finally full grown and up and laying, and they had eggs coming out of their ears at her house, and when were we coming to get some more eggs? I practically wanted to proclaim a national holiday. I went immediately over to their little wood house at the end of a long, still very snowy, rutted drive and got my first dozen. And when I got home and said, "I've got Dawn's eggs!" it was terribly satisfying to see on Alex's face the look he normally reserves for artisanal beer. He knew he was going to get them for dinner. And he did, of course. We had asparagus and fried eggs and butter and Parmesan over potato puree, followed by a salad with walnut oil dressing. Glass of white wine for me, stout for him. And he gave that sigh I was waiting for, too.

This is how:

For the potato puree, peel as many potatoes as you think you'll want, and just cover them with water. Add as many peeled garlic cloves as you like, and a bay leaf—a sprig of thyme, if you have one lying around, is nice. Bring to a boil and cook gently until the potatoes are tender, then put them, the cooked garlic cloves, along with some of the potato water they cooked in, into a heatproof bowl.

Add a dollop of butter, if you like. Either mash with a masher or, if you like them smoother, puree with a hand mixer, adding more potato water as needed to make a puree as loose or as tight as you like. I like a loose one for this purpose—one that will spread out over the bottom of the plate and soak up any yolk that manages to make it past the asparagus. Salt and pepper to taste, and add a couple of scrapings of fresh nutmeg. Cover and keep warm in a low oven.

While all of this is going on, put some lettuce in a bowl, keep the walnut oil and lemon wedges handy next to it. Run a wedge of Parmesan down the side of the grater that gives you nice thin long slices. Hold these for later.

Put a pan of water large enough to hold the asparagus flat on to boil. Salt it. Add as much asparagus as you want. Boil briskly till you can pierce the asparagus on their ends easily with a knife. Lift them out onto a towel set on a heatproof plate and set in the oven with the puree.

Gently fry as many eggs as you like—I go for 2 a person. You can use whatever method you like. I personally like to heat the pan, throw some butter in, tip the eggs in from cups (that way I know they're not going to break in the pan), salt and pepper, clap a lid on, and instantly turn off the heat. I let them sit for about five minutes before I check and see if they're done the way I like them, which is with a quivering but cooked white and a liquid gold yolk. (You may feel differently about your egg cooking process, and I certainly wouldn't argue with anything that gets the job done.)

Now it gets fun. Spread warm potato puree on plates. Put the asparagus on top—they look nice if they're all facing the same way.

Lift the eggs and put them on top of the asparagus. Meanwhile, heat the egg pan again, and throw in a tablespoon of butter for each person while you arrange Parmesan slices on top of the asparagus. When the butter bubbles and turns brown (don't let it blacken), pour on top of the Parmesan/egg/asparagus edifice. Serve right away, preferably with a glass of white wine. Encourage guests to spear the egg yolks and let them run all over the rest of the plate.

Have at it.

When you've finished with that, toss the lettuce with a little salt and pepper and walnut oil and a squeeze of lemon. I like about a 2 to 1 proportion of walnut oil to lemon, but you'll have your own ideas. Serve that out on the same plates you served the asparagus on. In the unlikely event there is any yolk or potato left, the salad mingles with this quite nicely.

(And while we're at it, here's another recipe particularly good with Dawn's eggs. Make some duxelles, which are essentially the old mushrooms they mark down at the market, chopped finely and cooked for a long, slow time with butter, a little garlic, a little thyme, salt and pepper, till all the moisture cooks out of them, and they're an evil looking rich tasting mess. You can freeze these easily, and this dish is a breeze if you have. Cook some pasta, about ¼ pound for each person. Penne is nice for this. Whisk the freshest, best eggs you can find in a warm serving bowl big enough to hold the pasta—I reckon one egg per person. Salt and pepper. Add as much grated Parmesan as you feel like. Heat the duxelles with a little white wine and/or a little cream, depending on how you feel and what you've got. When the pasta's done, drain it—not too thoroughly, a little pasta water lubricates everything nicely—and toss with the eggs and

Parmesan and duxelles. Serve on warm plates with a glass of red wine
and a green salad to follow. Heaven. Really.)

Another thing to do with Dawn's eggs . . .

> Eggs poached in roast tomato/chipotle chile sauce.
> Black beans refried.
> Avocado/jalapeno/cilantro/scallion/lime salad.

For the sauce:

Take about a pound and a half of tomatoes, cut in half, roast at
250° for a couple of hours, till a little blackened on the edges.

Finely mince a small onion and two garlic cloves, sauté till soft in
a tablespoon of oil. Add the tomatoes, diced. Add a finely chopped
chipotle chile, and a couple of teaspoons of its sauce. If this needs a
little liquid, add some light beer.

Cook till lightly thickened.

Wrap some corn tortillas in foil and put in a 350° oven.

Put casserole, with cooked black beans that have been mashed
into hot oil in which onion and garlic has been fried, into oven to
warm while you do the rest.

Make four indentations in the sauce. Slide a raw egg into each
indentation. Turn heat on low, cover, leave for seven minutes.

Meantime, the salad: mince lots of cilantro, scallions, one seeded
jalapeno. Add diced avocado. Squeeze wedge of lime over all. Mix

with one tablespoon of bland oil. (I use sunflower, but flax oil would be another good choice, and even healthier.) Add salt.

When eggs are set, put tortillas on plates (two to a plate).

Spoon sauce and eggs onto them—careful not to break the eggs. Put beans on top of a little mound of lettuce if you like, garnish with avocado salad.

Very good with beer.

Even with expensive organic eggs, this meal shouldn't cost more than $3 for two.

And you sleep very well afterwards.

Another lovely thing to eat (among the many, many lovely things to eat that there are) is egg custard, and I mean savory egg custard, the kind that you serve in a little glass ramekin on the side of something light and healthy for dinner, not for dessert. Easy on the stomach, easy on the checkbook, easy on the eye. Looks tough to make, so you get a lot of credit from your loved ones as they dip a careful spoon through the stuff and savor the first tender bites on their collective tongue. Useful. Useful, easy, frugal, and good—I mean, really, what more do you want out of life, let alone dinner?

This is how:

For two people (for four, just double):

Beat two eggs with a half teaspoon of light oil and some salt. Add a quarter cup minced cilantro, more or less. Then, add slowly, beating as you do, three quarters of a cup of hot water. (This, according to Maggie Gin's original recipe, is what makes the custard so tender.)

Divide between two Pyrex custard cups. Then lower into a steamer basket set over a pot of boiling water. Steam for about ten minutes, till a toothpick inserted comes out clean. (You can cook this in one larger heatproof bowl, in which case I think it would take about fifteen minutes.)

Sprinkle custards with minced green onion. I drizzle some oyster sauce on top. You can sprinkle them with soy sauce instead—that's equally delicious. A tiny bit of sesame oil, if you like the taste, goes well, too.

There are just about a million permutations you can apply to this recipe, if you feel so inclined (add sautéed mushrooms, add cooked spinach, skip the Asian flavors altogether and add cheese, etc.), but I never seem to get beyond this one.

(We'd had an extra lavish meal type weekend, as it was the Beloved Husband's birthday, so this came as part of a pulling-ourselves-back-together type meal: steamed brown rice topped with sautéed cabbage and soy sauce, and avocado halves with lemon juice on the side. We both felt light and happy afterwards. Come to think of it, we'd both felt light and happy after his birthday dinner, which involved four courses, sourdough bread, a bottle of rosé champagne, wine and extra desserts, so the secret here, I guess, is not to do the same thing all the time. . .)

I try not to experiment with more than one new, unfamiliar kind of wild mushroom per year. I'm one of those hyper-cautious types who begins envisaging liver damage immediately on consumption (although I am also one of those types who is physically incapable of seeing a mushroom growing in the wild without speculating on how it would taste with garlic and cream). And there was this one particular kind of spongy bulgy thing that popped up in the woods, sometimes in huge numbers, that I'd had my eye on for some time. I'd been trained by a professional mushroom guy to recognize a similar one, so I knew this was a type of bolete . . . and I knew there are a limited amount of toxic boletes, and those will generally not kill you, just make you really, really sick. So, I figured, I had a good shot. I have, after all, three different mushroom books (the best by far is David Arora's *Mushrooms Demystified*—highly, highly recommended). At the very worst, I'd have an unpleasant gastro-intestinal experience. Which was not the most terrible thing that could happen.

Still, after gazing at the two huge, gnome-home specimens we found next to the spring, I was nervous, as usual. I knew for sure—I thought—that they were some kind of Slippery Jack. Edible for sure—I thought. And when they blued a little bit where I cut them on the stem, I was more sure—I thought. Douglas Fir loving, no red pores, fruiting most around Thanksgiving in the Pacific Northwest. Hah. Got you. "I'm absolutely sure about this one," I announced to Alex, who was, as usual before dinner, on the phone and the computer and the beer mug all at the same time.

"I was sure you were," he said amiably. I have a promise from him that he will never, ever, ever eat a wild mushroom before I've vetted it. Alex's tendency is to leap first and look to see how many stories down afterwards, and, as I hope to keep him well into old age, certain precautions must be taken.

I was sure all right. Still, I went back to the books—all of them—three more times and read about all the possible toxic species that might even remotely resemble those lying on my kitchen counter. There wasn't one that was even close. So I'm safe.

I think.

So I fry up a bit of the mushrooms, dry, with garlic salt, and then a little added butter, and we taste. Just a bit for each of us. Hours before dinner, so if there's anything wrong, boy, will we know about it before I make them into a meal. We taste. A little watery, which tells me how to cook them later. But meaty. And good. Really good.

They taste like the woods on a winter's day. Now I relax. I am a great believer in my body telling me when something's wrong. And what my body was saying was, "This is good. Thank you."

So I was happy about those mushrooms.

At dinner, this is what I did with them:

I peeled off the slimy top skin, and pared away the dirt on the stems. Then I diced them. Put a pan on the burner at medium high heat and then the mushrooms went in dry. I fried them till they were nice and crisp and brown on the outside, then I glugged in some extra virgin olive oil and a bunch of minced garlic . . . and a handful of minced parsley.

Salt and pepper. Let them cool.

For two of us, I beat six of the Egg Lady's eggs. More chopped parsley. Salt and pepper. Then I added the cooled mushrooms. Some grated Parmesan. Topped with more grated Parmesan.

Cleaned the mushroom pan. Preheated the broiler. Heated the pan to where a drop of water sizzles on the surface.

Glugged in some olive oil. Added the eggs. Lifted them up, let them run around the pan. Cooked on lower heat till they were browned on the bottom. Slid them under the broiler till browned on top.

Wild mushroom omelet.

We had this with thin sliced potatoes cooked over high heat in duck fat. Tomatoes roasted for a couple of hours. A big salad with mesclun, walnuts, scallions, and blue cheese.

And we were very happy. As of this writing, still no liver damage. So that's another mushroom species happily identified as completely edible, and my forays into the natural world continue, with anticipation and the greatest, greatest, greatest possible respect . . .

While walking in the woods behind the house, and thinking about our dinner as a way of anchoring my thoughts in general, I couldn't decide between cold soba noodles with a radish salad, or something to do with cheese and broccoli. It was a very hot day, very humid, with the promise of thunderstorms clearly behind it. And there in front of me, having sprouted up that morning, was a log covered with oyster mushrooms.

I know oyster mushrooms. They and morels are the two wild

mushrooms I do know very well. And know how well they taste, too.

That decided it. For dinner we had:

Oyster mushrooms salad with baby kale and daikon leaves.

Broccoli tian with onions and Cheddar cheese.

Here's how to make the salad:

Take however many mushrooms you have, of any type (wild is best), and, having gotten rid of the grit and sliced them into manageable sizes, throw them into a hot pan in which butter and olive oil have heated. On top, throw much minced garlic and chopped scallions. Salt now (don't stint; mushrooms need salt). When the mushrooms have cooked, squeeze lemon on top of it. Then throw a lot of chopped parsley into it. And add a few glurgs of cream.

When all of this has amalgamated, toss with hardy lettuce leaves, like baby kale, or escarole, or turnip tops, or baby chard, or a sturdy mesclun mix. (If you want to use lighter lettuces—lamb's lettuce, butter lettuce, etc.—dress the leaves lightly with oil and lemon juice, and put the mushrooms on top, rather than mixing them in.)

Serve IMMEDIATELY, with a glass of red wine, and eat very, very slowly.

Follow by whatever course you think best. As, come to think of it, one should always do in life when one can.

The Mushroom Man at the Growers' Market always has something fascinating on his table, and whether it's because of the mysterious quality of the various fungi, or the fact that I know he's foraged for all of it in the mountains ringing the valley, or something else entirely, every week I'm absolutely riveted by the display. I spend a lot of time mooning about what I might do with those trompettes des morts, those hedgehog mushrooms, those morels.

One spring week, I stopped to greet him and eye his wares as usual, and halfway through a sentence my eyes widened. There was a heap of little marble-sized, dirt covered balls, and a sign that said: Oregon truffles.

"Not really," I said.

"They won't be here long," he said.

Now I'd heard we grew truffles in Oregon, and I'd seen them in the mushroom books, and I'd been more than a little entranced by the general romance of them. I'd only ever eaten fresh truffles once, in creamy scrambled eggs at La Regalade, in the 14th, in Paris—at which meal I was so overwhelmed by the huge terrine on the table, and the wine the couple at the next-door table offered us from their bottle, and the guys on the other side of me tucking into what looked like an entire steer, that I hardly took in a separate truffle flavor. But of course it's the legend of truffles that's the important thing. I mean, if you've read Colette, or Joseph Wechsberg, on the subject, truffles stay with you forever as a kind of fairy tale. A European myth. So the idea that they were here in Oregon, too—there was a certain quiet satisfaction in that. Or, as Thoreau so pertinently said, "I walk not toward Europe, but toward Oregon."

So I bought one. Of course I bought one.

I told the Mushroom Man I was going to cook it in creamy soft scrambled Egg Lady eggs, and he thoroughly approved of that. He told me to hold out my hand, and then he pressed a knuckle and said, "That's how they feel now." Then he pressed the skin between my knuckles, and said, "That's how they feel when they're ready to eat. They're ready about 12 days after I've picked them. And they don't wait for you! You eat when the truffle is ready, okay?"

No question, I said. I always eat when the food in question is ready. It's part of my partnership agreement with the Good Life. He nodded and put the small black thing into a little plastic container and handed it over with a certain solemnity.

The next day I smelled the truffle. It smelled faintly sweet, but nothing very overwhelming, and I put it away again. But two days later, it smelled intensely of . . . what? Of nothing else I could think of. Something familiar, but nothing I could name. Violet pastilles, I thought, but that wasn't quite it either. I was a little taken aback by this—I'd somehow imagined something musky, something a little more earthy and less perfumed. Well, it was earthy. But not in the way I'd thought. Not like mushrooms. More like . . . cheese and hay.

By the next day, the violet smell was even stronger, crossed with a kind of smell of green grass and wet dirt. I felt the truffle thoughtfully and decided I probably had about two more days before it got to where the Mushroom Man said it should. So the next day, I took out a little nailbrush I keep for cleaning mushrooms and scrubbed the truffle till it looked like a speckled malted milk ball. The smell kept rising up off it, and our little dog licked my hands with special enthusiasm after, even after I washed them. Then I minced half of it up finely and mixed with 5 of Dawn's eggs and 1 egg yolk, for them to sit and soak up the flavors overnight.

I saved the other half of the truffle. Half of that we had grated over that night's pasta and butter and cheese, and the aroma was definite, though more elusive than I liked. I'd made a mistake by putting a lot of parsley in the sauce, and that made everything too complex; you could almost catch the truffle taste, but then it would fly off in a different direction. With all that parsley in there you couldn't quite separate the flavor out. So I wouldn't make that mistake the next night.

The next night would be strictly butter and eggs and cream and truffles. As for the remaining quarter of raw truffle, that I planned to grate on the eggs after they were done, to be warmed by their heat alone.

So the next night, with a certain sense of occasion and curiosity, I opened a bottle of rosé. Poured out a glass. Got the egg bowl out of the fridge. When I lifted the lid, the smell flowered up at me. It was startling, the power of it. And what was in it, I wondered? What was that scent? Violets, for sure—but violets mixed with ripe cheese and hay. That's about the best way I can describe it. I pondered this briefly, along with the beautiful black and gold marble of the truffled eggs. Then I shook myself, and got down to business. I smeared a lot of butter around the inside of an earthenware cazuela I'd brought back from Spain. I put that on a flame tamer, and, pouring the eggs in, I turned the heat on low.

Meanwhile, I toasted four big pieces of local sourdough bread, and kept them warm in the oven.

I put a salad ready to be tossed on the table—dressing of lemon, thyme, garlic, walnut oil, blue cheese, with diced avocado and toasted hazelnuts in the bottom of the bowl; salad spoon and fork crisscrossed on top; mesclun leaves heaped on top of those.

I stirred the eggs pretty continuously for about twenty minutes, until they were a creamy amalgam—at one point adding a glug of cream to slow the cooking down, and finishing them with a tablespoon or two of butter cut up and stirred till melted, so we're not talking a spa dinner here—and then I poured them on the bread and grated what was left of the truffle on top.

Alex's eyes got wide after he took the first bite. "This doesn't taste like anything I've ever eaten before," he said. "What about you?" I laughed, because all of a sudden I was back at La Regalade, and now I knew what that elusive flavor was I'd been too over stimulated at the time to take in then.

"Yes," I said. "Just one other time."

And we talked about Oregon, and how glad we are to live here, and I had another glass of rosé, and the night went quickly, too quickly, which is the way it's supposed to be with good nights, I guess.

Salads

When Alex asked me what I wanted him to grow in the garden this year, I rather thoughtlessly said, "You can't have enough lettuce or greens." This was only the third year of his garden, and in previous years, the lettuce grew rather meagerly, if sweetly. A lettuce plant in Al's garden was almost always small before it bolted, and it was so tender that I couldn't bear to do anything to it but dress it with just a capful of walnut oil right before we ate it. It wilted so fast, that lettuce, that I wouldn't dress it till Alex was sitting at the table.

It's like eating air, eating baby lettuces from the garden—albeit air with a nice green smell.

But this year . . . he mulched and hoed and enriched, and Lord knows what all, and then the weather has been alternately hot, then rainy, then hot again, and Alex has been away for a month, and here I am with a garden just full of lettuces and greens of all kinds, growing up to a foot tall.

I still maintain you can't have enough of it, though.

So I have steamed turnip greens and rice for lunch. Sautéed daikon greens with garlic and oyster sauce wrapped in whole wheat tortillas that have been smeared with hoisin sauce. Miso soup with shredded holland greens. And gombo zhèbes, from John Thorne's *Serious Pig*, which is just about every green in the garden, cooked with just about every herb, scallions, jalapeno, garlic, and some bacon. I had that with toast and cheese. Then leftovers for lunch on corn tortillas with shredded lettuce and grated carrot and shredded Monterey Jack.

But the salads are the most amazing. Mizuna with a soy sauce dressing. Chicory and rocket with blue cheese. Lamb's lettuce with walnut oil and lemon juice. And so on.

These are my three favorite salad dressings in no particular order:

1.) Blue Cheese dressing: either crush or mash a garlic clove. Salt and pepper. One part red wine or sherry vinegar. A little dried mustard. Three parts good olive oil. Add crumbled blue cheese and mash some of it in.

This is particularly good with hardy lettuces—chicory and rocket or romaine, for example. Chopped scallions and toasted walnuts bring it to God.

2.) Lemon/Thyme/Soy: one crushed or mashed garlic clove. Crushed dried or fresh thyme. Salt and pepper. One part lemon juice, two parts light oil (I use sunflower or walnut). A little soy to taste.

This is great on mizuna, or mixed leaf, or beet tops, or oak leaf, anything a little lighter than the hardy lettuces, but not light as a cloud.

3.) Mustard vinaigrette: One crushed or mashed garlic clove. Salt and pepper. One part red wine vinegar mixed with one part Dijon mustard. Three parts olive oil whisked in.

Best with hardy greens, like the ones with Blue Cheese dressing. In fact, I'm having it for dinner tonight, with chicory and rocket, next to my macaroni and cheese . . .

Alex was so delighted that he could grow tomatillos and chilies almost without trying that we ended up with a tomatillo and chile plantation outside. He apologetically brought in whole armloads of them, for awhile there.

This overabundance led me to a tomatillo breakthrough. The usual way to deal with them is to make salsa. But how much green salsa do you really need? I've always liked them as a salad, as Diana Kennedy suggests (just chop them roughly, toss with chopped cilantro, onion, a serrano chile, some salt and olive oil, and top with crumbled white cheese). But these ones I had in front of me were so tart and so green still that they needed . . . something. And besides, we were having them with broiled teriyaki salmon and black rice, and I wanted to make a nod to that.

So I chopped about twenty of them roughly, put them in a bowl with chopped cilantro, chopped scallions, a chopped serrano, salt, some light olive oil.

I looked at them, brooding. Too tart, I thought. Then I had an inspiration. So I diced an avocado and added it.

Still too tart.

That was when the breakthrough happened.

Fish sauce. Nuoc mam, nam pla, whatever. Vietnamese or Filipino, made out of you probably don't want to know what, but absolutely killer added at the right time and place—and you'd never notice it, just what it does. (Buy it in an Asian market; it's cheap and lasts forever.)

I added a teaspoon and tossed. And Alex had thirds.

If you find yourself with some tomatoes that are almost good, but not quite what they should be, and some rocket that is almost past it, there is, I've found, hope. Not only hope, but absolute, positive, delicious salad in the offing.

Take the tomato. Dice it. Toss it with balsamic vinegar and olive oil in a one to one ratio. (If I'm going to add enough rocket for two people—a couple of handfuls—I use one teaspoon of each; if enough for four people, one tablespoon of each.) Salt. You can add a halved garlic clove if you like; it's good with or without.

NOW . . . here's the key . . . mince a branch or two of marjoram . . . or a handful of basil . . . or a branch of oregano . . . and add.

The marjoram's the nicest. But you'll have to grow it yourself, unless the herb department at your grocery is more creative than mine.

Let this marinate for an hour or so. More is fine. Less is acceptable.

About a half hour before dinner, chop your handfuls of rocket and throw in with the tomatoes. Toss. Leave to wilt and marinate.

This is great served on the same plate with something that will mingle with the tomato juices. One night we had it with wagon wheels tossed with olive oil and garlic and lots of minced parsley. Another, with potato salad made with sour cream vinaigrette and huge handfuls of chopped parsley and dill. It was perfect with both.

It was really one of those perfect dinners, where almost everything comes out of the ground around the house, and you feel light and happy afterward. It was only a beet salad followed by a Vegetable Ragout (turnips, carrots, yellow squash, onions, garlic, lettuce, peas, marjoram) and bread and goat cheese . . . but those meals are the best, you know? The most . . . I'm not sure how to put it . . . the ones I'm the most conscious when I'm making and the most conscious when I'm eating. The ones that make me the most aware that I'm alive, and that it's not going to last very long, and that I had better make the most of it for myself and anyone I get near while it does. I'm almost hesitating to call it a sacrament, but, what the hell, go for it—that's just what it is. The preparation and eating of the meal.

You can't do better sacramentally than a good beet salad.
Here's how:

A bunch of beets with their greens.

Separate greens from the beets. Scrub the beets, wrap them in aluminum foil, stick them in a really hot—450°—oven for about 50 minutes. Use a toaster oven if you've got nothing else going, both to save energy and heat in the kitchen. (If you're cooking something else in the big oven, just shove the beets in there, no matter what the temperature . . . just allow extra time if the temp is less.) I do this in the afternoon for a salad for the evening.

Make a vinaigrette. Mash a garlic clove, add 1 tablespoon sherry vinegar (or any vinegar, really), salt, pepper . . . let this sit about five minutes, then add 3 tablespoons olive oil.

When beets are done, wait till cool enough to handle, then peel. If they're done, the peel should just slide off with a little finger action. Either dice or slice, and put in a bowl. Mix with the vinaigrette. Toss with chopped herbs—I used parsley and basil the last time I made this, but mint is great, dill good, chervil fantastic . . . and so on. Scallions are good, too, if you like them.

Meanwhile, wash and de-stem the beet greens. Shred them.

Put another garlic clove in the mortar, mash it, add a tablespoon of vinegar, a little salt and pepper.

Right before dinner, heat a tablespoon of olive oil in a skillet. Toss in the still damp beet greens, toss over medium high heat till wilted and done, add the vinegar/garlic mixture and toss till it smells divine.

On each plate, put a line of beet greens and a mound of beets.

Serve.

Keep the troubles of the world in your head, but talk, during dinner, from your heart. It makes for better digestion, I find.

I wanted to make a brandade of salt cod and potato for dinner—Easter dinner, in fact. The classic accompaniment is salad, and I was out of greens. What else would go? We're half an hour from the nearest market, and I loathe just popping into a market for one or two things even in the best of circumstances, so there was nothing for it but to figure out another way forward. Fortunately, this kind of challenge always gets me going. And I wasn't going to give up on the brandade. It was a holiday, after all, and of course I had a bottle of Spanish rosé sparkling wine chilling in the fridge, perfect with the brandade . . . I just needed a damned salad.

Now the market problem had given me not just one, but two bunches of beautiful parsley—one curly, one Italian flat—in the fridge. This was the result of the Husband's buying what he thought was one parsley, one cilantro. Being a canny and happy wife, I didn't mention the mistake, just complimented him on the general beauty of the herbs (vibrant green leaves, nice juicy stems), and gave some serious thought as to how to use all that parsley.

It turns out it makes a terrific salad. And just the thing for brandade. If you like garlic, you can garlic up both of them as much as you want; if you don't, don't. They're both still good without it. Though in my opinion, nothing is as good without garlic as it would have been with.

Here's how:

I used James Beard's recipe as a guideline, but I'm not convinced you really have to finely mince the garlic and let it sit in the dressing for two hours, the way he suggests. If you do it my way, you don't have to think so far ahead.

Mash a clove of garlic into one part vinegar, salt and pepper, add three parts oil. The usual vinaigrette, in fact. Beard's right that sherry vinegar tastes terrific with parsley, and since it tastes terrific with brandade, too, it was the choice for that dinner. (An extra bonus, it looked terrific on the plate. In fact, the whole dinner looked terrific . . . the gold white of the brandade curling around the jade green parsley, and the rose colored wine on the side . . .)

To make the salad, just strip the parsley leaves off their stems. I used two-thirds curly parsley to about one third flat, but the next day for lunch I used all curly to great effect . . . and in a way, I think that second salad was even better. That time I sliced a shallot very thinly and let it sit in one part raspberry vinegar (salt and pepper, too) for about an hour. This really is important. The shallot tastes much sweeter after the soak; you can taste the difference yourself if you try it both ways. Then I added three parts light walnut oil. I used this salad as a topping for some beans I'd experimented with . . . using bouillabaisse seasoning for a vegetarian version of baked beans . . . they were okay, but not really worth passing the recipe around. But with the parsley salad lumped on top of them and a warmed whole wheat tortilla, they made a very passable lunch indeed.

And by the way, if you make this, don't throw away the stems. Just tie them together and use them to flavor a soup or a broth, or a stew, or...I chop them up and put them in my dogs' food, myself...

There was a spring blizzard here the other day, when my refrigerator was at the end of its shopping cycle and relatively bare— this meant the mountain pass between me and the market was an icy mess, and not really worth crossing to get a handful of lettuce for the evening meal.

So.

I had plenty of cupboard stuff, and planned some fettuccine with cream and butter and smoked salmon with a splash of whisky, and all the parsley left from last week's shopping, minced finely and thrown in. But what to eat with that?

We had one lone avocado left in the onion basket. A shallot that had escaped my notice, bought, I think, around Christmas time.

And in the refrigerator, a bowl of three halves of roasted plum tomatoes.

I try to have a bowl of these hanging about all the time in the winter, since they last forever, and they are exactly what to do with winter tomatoes that don't have much taste. You just buy a bunch of Romas when they're on special, slice them in half, and put them on a foil covered cookie sheet, and sprinkle them with a little coarse salt, and shove them in a 200° oven . . . then forget about them for hours. Two hours, even three. When they're done, they're leathery and chewy and taste delicious, and you can just throw them in a bowl and leave them there to be used at will.

This was the dressing I made from that:

For two people:

Slice the shallot thinly. Put it in a bowl with 1 teaspoon of sherry vinegar and a little salt. LET SIT FOR AT LEAST FIFTEEN MINUTES. (Very important—it completely changes the taste of the shallot.)

Right before serving, dice one and a half roasted Roma tomatoes finely and add.

Stir in 1 tablespoon olive oil.

Slice one ripe avocado in half, spoon dressing over both halves, and serve on the side of something savory and rich.

(For more people, just multiply the ingredients.)

A friend of mine died, and the dinner I cooked a few nights later was absolute crap. Every single thing came out bad. The cauliflower cheese burned on top, the sauce thinned out unpleasantly. The potatoes tasted mushy and bland. I overcooked the asparagus. If anything was needed to convince me that cooking is an expression of how you feel in yourself and your body, of how solidly you're linked to the earth and to your own deepest needs and desires, that did it.

I could see my body running away from the basic facts of my life, because those basic facts killed my friend, and then would kill me. So I didn't enjoy cooking. I didn't enjoy eating. All the connections in my circuitry went awry.

And I think that is the way things are. I don't think you can change that. But I think you look it in the eye, and you give yourself and your body a break and you wake up every day feeling a little differently about it, going back and forth, one bad day, one a little better, one worse, one inexplicably happy. The usual process of healing after any kind of a wound. Then you notice you've come back to yourself and to the world and to life, and you figure that you're damn lucky to have the time you do have. And you were lucky to have the time you had with your friend.

That happened, too.

So I'll give you a recipe I made for him when he was alive.

He was a most confirmed man-about-town, and there was never much to speak of in the way of edibles in his tiny, utterly chaotic kitchen. Dining out, you see: a way of life. Alex and I would always stay with him when we were in London, and he would always dine out with us. But when I travel, after awhile I get utterly sick of dining out. Especially when I'm dining out in indifferent places, known more for their decor and clientele than for the love they put into their food. So one night, I just balked.

"I'll cook us something to eat in front of the telly, so we don't have to go out. Whatever you've got in the kitchen, I'll conjure something up."

My friend looked at me, appalled. "There IS nothing in that kitchen!"

"Hmmm," I said. "Well, we'll see." I settled him and Alex down with a couple of beers and went to forage.

As I recall, I didn't make anything particularly noteworthy that evening, but I did manage to keep us all from starvation, based on some dusty boxes of exotic dried pasta, a gift bottle of expensive olive oil from his favorite Italian restaurant, a couple of packets of macadamia nuts, and—surprise!—the herbs I found growing ornamentally in his garden ("didn't even know they were there, let alone edible!" he said).

The next time we came to stay, and I opened the refrigerator to get a bottle of white wine, there they were. Four eggplant.

I went into the living room. "Ahem," I said. My friend pretended not to hear. "Why are there four eggplant in your refrigerator? And, might I add, a head of garlic sitting on the counter?"

"I LOVE eggplant! I eat it ALL the time!"

I grinned at that. The vision of my friend, nattily attired, cooking himself up an eggplant for supper. But I got the message. And went out shopping for the few things I could pick up down the street. I made a bunch of salads. The best of the lot was the eggplant caviar.

Here's how:

Prick however many eggplants you have with a fork so they don't explode while they cook. Put them on a foil lined cookie sheet in a 400° oven until they've softened and crumpled—probably about 30 to 45 minutes. It won't matter much if they overcook a little, but you don't want to undercook them.

When they're done, bring them out and let them cool. Just enough so you can handle them without burning yourself. They taste better if they soak up the fixings while they're still warm.

If you want, you can make a dressing in a bowl while you wait. Either that, or just add all these disparate ingredients, one by one, to the eggplant when you've chopped it up, then taste for seasoning. I do it either way. It depends how I feel.

That night I probably split the eggplant in half, scooped and scraped the pulp out into a bowl, mashed it about, splashed olive oil in to moisten it. Then I added minced garlic, some chopped capers I'd found in the back of a cupboard, the squeezings of a lemon I'd bought from the newsagent's around the corner, some Maldon salt to taste. And then lots and lots of chopped parsley and mint I found growing on the flower bed borders in the garden.

We had this with warmed up pita bread, also bought at the newsagent's, as I recall.

It was a very jolly evening indeed. Eggplant caviar for our friend Hercules. It makes me sad and happy to think about, both at the same time.

Salads

The first spring Alex had a garden, every morning, before he'd even made the morning coffee and tea, he'd be off outside, peering down at the little green shoots, willing them taller and stronger. Both of us held our breath—we could hardly wait—till the early rows of lettuce had grown just enough so that I could carefully harvest the larger leaves one by one: the mizuna, and the baby chard, the arugula, the marjoram, the salad burnet, the thyme, the oregano, the greens from the daikon radish. Now that spring was here, the light stayed out longer, and it had that gentle beginning quality that comes from being filtered through the new pale green leaves. I would go out in it with a wide white and rose colored porcelain bowl and pick a salad for dinner.

The first time I did this—well, I don't remember anymore what we had after. But I will remember that salad until I die . . . I think it likely that if I'm conscious as I die, I'll remember that salad on purpose, with love, and think of the beautiful things we have in this life.

I threw a little bit of gray sea salt on the leaves and tossed them gently with just a teaspoon of toasted walnut oil. I served it on wide white plates, just as the sun was fading behind the trees, and Alex said, "What is this dressing? It's the most delicious one I've ever had." And of course the deliciousness came from the garden, and from his love of the garden, and from my love of cooking from the garden, and from our love of being together there eating those delicate, fairy-like greens in the early spring silence.

155

Cooking By the Seat
of Your Pants

It made me a little sad, and a little frustrated, to read a newspaper article called something like: "Secrets of Home Cooks Who Don't Use Recipes." I mean, it was well intentioned, but its subtext was "this is something mysterious that they know and you don't." For something so simple—so basic—it made it all complicated and scary and exclusive, like a secret society that wouldn't have me as a member.

Ach, I thought to myself. Aren't people's lives tough enough without constantly telling them that they don't know how to take care of themselves?

The "secrets" were all things like: "I grew up on a farm and we had fresh fruit and vegetables." Or "My mother/grandmother/ mysterious gypsy woman passing by taught me all the traditional recipes." But you know, I grew up in an early Sixties city, and we had perfectly horrible food from the grocery store—prepackaged and factory everything, unripe fruit, deflavorized vegetables, squishy bread, bright orange cheese. My mother hated to cook during those years, the years of her slavery to the bland tastes of five kids (except for me, who she still marvels at for preferring pickled herring to ice cream from the very start). We certainly never shared warm moments at the stove preparing foodstuffs from the old country. In fact, the one dish she made most often, which I always fondly assumed WAS a traditional dish of exotic Macao—chicken legs baked with butter and soy sauce—turned out to be, to my great amusement, one of the dishes the women's magazines of the time used to promote as quick 'n' tasty for your kids. It was, too. But it wasn't the kind of dish a mother passes down to the daughter. Not an heirloom, if you know what I mean. (A great dish, though, and truly quick 'n' tasty, so for recipe see page 32.)

So I didn't have any of those essential advantages, and I didn't start out as a particularly good cook, either. But I don't cook with recipes. True, I read them for fun, but I don't pay much attention to them. And I'm a pretty good cook now. At least, my loved ones and my friends enjoy what I cook, and what more do I want?

Here are my secrets for cooking without recipes. Know what you want to eat. Keep it simple. Enjoy yourself. Come to think of it, those are my secrets for having a good life, too.

That knowing what you want to eat is the most important. It's amazing how hard it is to know that. When you think about it, it's the root of a lot of aimless misery, that not knowing what we want. So I spend a little time on it, thinking about what would really taste good from what I have, and what would really make me happy. (One of my wonderful sisters-in-law once told me that her family hated cilantro, but she had a real craving for it one night, so she said the hell with it, and made Arroz con Pollo with lots of the loathed herb. It was their favorite dinner, and now they have it all the time. I've had it, too. And it's really, really good.)

The other night, I was alone and a little blue. When I get that way, I think eggs. I like huevos rancheros, and I like them with tomatillo salsa. You can use the stuff in a bottle or a can, but we happened to have a burgeoning crop of fresh ones in the garden right then, so I took three or four big ripe ones off the vine, plucked a serrano chile, and tossed the husked tomatillos and the seeded chile in the food processor with a scallion, a garlic clove, and a few sprigs of cilantro. Pureed the whole thing.

(Now here's where I made a mistake—before tasting it, I added a little sugar. But these tomatillos were riper than the ones I usually cook with, and now the sauce was too sweet. So what? I added a little lime juice and reminded myself not to be so nonchalant in the future.)

Then I fried a tortilla in a little oil till it was limp, fished it out and drained it on a paper towel, and poured the salsa into the pan. Cooked it about five minutes briskly till it was cooked down and thick. Tasted for salt again. Then, turning the heat down low, I broke a nice egg into the sauce and covered the pan. Cooked it for about five minutes till the white was set and the yolk still runny. Turned it out onto the drained tortilla, topped it with a sliced avocado, sat down at the table and got to it.

And I cheered up, even though that salsa was a little too sweet.

There were a million different things I could have done to that salsa. I could have cooked the tomatillos and chile in boiling water first. I could have added an onion instead of a scallion. I could have skipped the garlic. Or, like I said, I could have used a salsa somebody else made for me. It wouldn't have mattered. All that mattered, really, was that I thought about what I wanted to eat, and then I cooked it, and then I enjoyed myself when I ate it. That's when you know that your life is in your own hands, you know? And that feeling really does take root in you and spreads out . . . oh, all over the place, into places where you least expect it.

I like leftovers, myself. They're not just stuff cluttering up the refrigerator, they're a challenge. I like meditating on how to make them even more alluring the second time around, with the least amount of hassle possible, and when I manage both of those, I get a real feeling of satisfaction.

Some things are easy. Refried beans, for example. Reheat them, plop them on top of grated carrot and shredded cabbage on a heated whole wheat tortilla, top them with grated cheese and diced avocado and green onions and a dollop of sour cream, maybe a little salsa if I have it, and that's lunch.

Cooked rice. Fried with any bits of onion and cilantro and veggies around, and an egg mixed in, served with soy sauce. Or fried with slices of garlic, then eggs steamed on top.

Cold fish. Tossed with freshly cooked lentils, and parsley, and grated carrot, and either a vinaigrette or mayonnaise.

Leftover omelet. Sliced and put on toast that's been covered with mayonnaise, served with a little salad.

Any roasted vegetables. Dice up, sauté an onion with butter and a little curry powder, add diced cooked vegetables, a little wine, a couple of cups of water, some pasta (or leftover diced potato, or leftover rice, come to think of it), cook till pasta is tender and all the flavors mingle, salt and pepper—nice veggie soup.

And so on.

Some refrigerator landscapes, of course, are more of a challenge than others. For example, the other day. One small bowl of leftover vegetable stew. One helping of cold whole wheat fusilli tossed with sautéed onions, soy sauce, and parsley. A little bit of leftover grated Romano cheese. A helping of sliced fennel tossed with lemon and olive oil. One lone kohlrabi lurking in the vegetable bin.

So this is what I did.

I put the pasta in a heatproof shallow dish and covered with the Romano cheese. Foil on top, in the toaster oven at 350° for about twenty minutes, or until the pasta was warmed through and the cheese melted. I heated up the veggie stew in a little pan. I peeled the kohlrabi and sliced it from the bottom to the top. (I got in the habit of getting kohlrabi when we lived in England, where the Asian markets sell a lot of young, tender ones in the spring. That's where I learned you slice it bottom to top, instead of side to side . . . the tender bit is at one end, and that way you get a little of everything. I highly recommend raw kohlrabi. It tastes like very sweet peeled broccoli stem, if that appeals to you—it does to me, very much—and when I can get them, we eat them with drinks, before dinner.)

Then I put a few lettuce leaves on plates, with a couple of slices of lemon. The heated, now really thick, stew went on top of half of the lettuce. The fennel salad went on top of the other half. The heated pasta went on the side. The kohlrabi piled up against the pasta.

That was a satisfying meal. It looked good, tasted good, and I had the smug feeling that comes from melding odds and ends into a good lunch, and getting that space back out of the refrigerator besides.

(A few days later, lunch was another leftovers personal best, if I do say so myself. Heated spelt tortillas—yes, they sound nutty and New Age-y, but they're delicious, especially for all you gluten allergists out there—topped with grated carrot, then a layer of heated leftover-from-dinner salt cod stew—onions, salt cod, tomatoes, Spanish paprika, chile pepper, garlic, chard, and diced potato—topped with dollops of garlic mayonnaise. Lemon slices on the side.)

I love casseroles. That's not what we call them now; they've been upgraded . . . or rather, since the word casserole got more or less degraded during its sad period of being adulterated with cans of mushroom soup and crushed potato chips on top, I guess we've re-branded them. The cookbooks call them "gratins" now, which is French, as far as I can tell, for casserole. Or tians. But they're casseroles just the same. Which means they transform individual potentially boring items in your refrigerator into something rich and strange, and they do it while you're doing something else before dinner.

Basically, what they are—what they all are—is some version of starch layered with some version of cooked vegetables and/or meat covered with some version of milk/cheese/eggs and browned bread crumbs. In almost infinite permutation. There's always some version that will meet whatever are the evening's needs.

So here were my needs. I didn't want to fuss. I wanted something that would cook a long time without needing attention, and something that would use what was left in a near empty larder. I had fresh mushrooms and carrots, and a bowl of leftover brown rice. I had frozen spinach, which is always nice to have in the house, and I had a lot of butter and milk, which I keep extras of in the winter, when I might not be able to get to town because of the weather. The snow was breaking up, and I wanted to clear that out of the freezer.

I had some cheese. (I always have some cheese.) And I had a yogurt container full of frozen breadcrumbs. I make these when the loaf gets down to the end, and I'm afraid it'll mold before we finish it. Just toss in the food processor, give it a few pushes, and then decant into a freezer container. They last forever, have a million uses, and you have the satisfying feeling of not having thrown away what would have been good bread.

First, when I contemplated those ingredients, I felt a mild irritation that I didn't have any eggs. My casseroles—tians—generally get held together by a mixture of eggs and milk.

That was when I remembered Béchamel sauce. White sauce when it's at home. Béchamel sauce is a wonder. It's homey and exotic, all at the same time. It reminds you of your grandmother's cooking, and it intimates that your grandmother might have grown up in a small town near Dijon. You just about always have the basic ingredients— milk, butter, flour, sometimes a little cream. And it dresses everything up without making a fuss about it, like the one scarf or the one belt that makes it so you can wear your jeans to the party and not look like you just wore them to clean house.

So this is what I did.

In a regular enameled saucepan, I made the Béchamel. This stuff is much hardier than they let on in most recipe books (isn't everything?),

163

and you don't have to worry yourself too much over it. I melted 3 tablespoons of butter over low heat, and added the same amount of flour. Cooked it gently, not letting it brown, but cooking the flour taste out, for about fifteen minutes. Then I added—slowly—1½ cups of milk. (The recipes always tell you to heat the milk or risk lumps. I don't bother, and I've never had a problem. You just whisk it in slowly, whisking lumps as they appear, or even long after they've appeared. It'll stay tame if you show it who's boss in a cheerful way. As, come to think of it, with most things in life.) I left that to simmer while I assembled the rest of the ingredients.

First I melted about a tablespoon of butter in a large-ish skillet, then added the breadcrumbs, enough to cover the eventual top layer of my casserole. I stirred these around until they turned a nice golden brown, then emptied them into a bowl I found in the back of the fridge that held a little grated Romano leftover from a previous dinner. Then I mopped out the skillet with a paper towel, and used that to grease an oval glass casserole dish. (You can use any shape dish you want; I like a shallow one because I like bits of the casserole to cook crispy and brown—my favorite part.)

I added more butter to the skillet, and sautéed about fifteen sliced mushrooms. Salt and pepper. The frozen spinach, a whole ten-ounce package, got dumped in still frozen when the mushrooms were browned. It didn't take much to defrost it and mingle it, lightly cooked, with the mushrooms.

Then I grated some fresh nutmeg over the spinach and mushrooms. While I was at it, I tasted the Béchamel, salted and peppered it, and grated some fresh nutmeg in it, too. If you don't like nutmeg, you can skip this, of course. But I highly recommend it, myself.

Somewhere in here, I cut some Swiss cheese into small dice. Mixed that with the bowl of leftover rice.

When the Béchamel was thick and suave and tasted good, I poured in a little cream I'd had in the freezer. (Like with the bread, I buy a big thing of cream, and if we're not going to finish it by the due date, pour it into a container and freeze it. Very useful for those nights when you want to have potatoes cooked in cream, or a little cream for a soup, or . . . or. . .) Then I turned off the heat, and stirred in the rice and cheese.

Now I layered the casserole. You can do this anyway you like, or you can mix everything together. Last night I did it this way: a layer of rice/cheese/Béchamel on the bottom of the dish. A layer of the spinach and mushrooms. A top layer of rice etc. Then I spread the breadcrumbs and Romano across the top to brown.

I was kind of sorry I didn't have any lettuce for a salad, when I remembered all those carrots on the bottom shelf of the refrigerator. Now, I usually steam my carrots, and then brown them with a little butter and brown sugar at the last minute before dinner, but I wanted to spend the next forty minutes having a quiet glass of wine in front of the fire with my husband, not fussing in the kitchen. So instead I peeled and sliced thinly as many carrots as I thought we could eat, tossed them in another casserole dish with a tablespoon of butter, a little brown sugar, a pinch of ground ginger, salt, pepper, and a tablespoon of water. I turned on the oven to 350º, and shoved the carrots in to start warming up with the oven. (You can cover the carrots so they steam, but check them halfway through cooking—if there's too much liquid, take the lid off and let it cook away. They're best when they're a little browned around the edges.)

While I waited for that, I chopped a bit of parsley. It took about fifteen minutes for the oven to get up to speed, which gave the carrots a head start on the casserole, and when I knew it was hot enough, I added the parsley to the carrots, and put the casserole in next to them.

Then I went off happily to have my glass of wine.

About forty-five minutes later I checked up on the food. I didn't even need to set a timer; the smells wafting toward us were enough. It was all done, but it was fine to leave it in longer, especially if, like me, you like everything a little crispy and browned. And as we were right in the middle of an interesting conversation, I poured a little more wine in my glass and went back to the fire.

It was a lovely dinner. It might seem a little sparse, only the two dishes. And you might not like that, and want to add baked chicken, or a first course of boiled artichokes and mayonnaise, or whatever you like. But it was perfect for that moment for us, and it looked pretty too—the green and brown and white of the casserole, next to the orange and green of the carrots on the white plates. The sweetness of the carrots was just the thing next to the richness of the casserole. And there was a little casserole left over to have for lunch on another day.

Sometimes I don't trust recipes. I look at them with misgivings and think to myself something like "5 ounces of Gorgonzola cheese per person? And no butter?" Then I start muttering like a witch and fussing about with the ingredients on my own bat. And every so often I find out, well, really, if it's a trustworthy writer, I was wrong and the writer was right.

Anyway, I was in a bit of an argument with Nigel Slater the other night, and I have to admit, he turned out correct. (He's almost right, too, that his is the best roast chicken in the world, although it's not as good as mine. He doesn't brine his. But that's another story.) I mean, I still fussed with the recipe, and altered it to suit what I had in the refrigerator, but basically, the guy was on solid ground. So I apologize for not believing in him utterly.

The recipe in question was for penne and broccoli and cheese. He suggested warming about 5 ounces of runny cheese per person in a big pasta bowl, then adding hot drained boiled broccoli and the pasta . . . a little cooking water to bind it . . . toss it together and eat in warmed bowls.

Well, I wasn't sure. Also I like to steam broccoli rather than boil it. Also I didn't have any Gorgonzola.

So this was what I did instead.

For two people:
I used a big pasta pot with a steamer insert (my modus operandi, as you may by now have guessed, always involves trying to cut steps/make fewer things to wash/make life as easy for myself as possible without endangering deliciousness). Preheated the oven to 175º, put a big ovenproof pasta bowl and two smaller bowls in. Brought a lot of water to the boil in the pasta pot. Meantime, I washed one bunch

of broccoli—about three good stalks—, peeled and diced the stems, detached the flowerets into similar small pieces and put the result in the steamer basket. When the water boiled, I salted it, added half a pound of penne pasta, fit the steamer basket with the broccoli on top and clapped on the lid. I set the timer for five minutes. Then I start checking the broccoli.

Then I chopped up a 3½ ounce goat cheese, grated a chunk of Asiago, and crumbled what was left of the end of some blue cheese. This was maybe about 6 ounces total, but I didn't get fussy about it. It was just what meltable cheese I had in the fridge, and what tasted good together on my mind's palate.

I threw these into the warming pasta bowl in the oven to soften. Added a bunch of freshly ground pepper.

The broccoli was beautifully done—tender and bright green—at five minutes, so I took it out, dumped it on top of the cheese in the pasta bowl, shoved that back in the oven, added a little oil to the penne so it wouldn't stick while it cooked, and set the timer for 3 more minutes. That's when I start checking the pasta for doneness.

While I stood there drinking a glass of wine, contemplating the whole thing, I started to worry I needed a little something to lubricate the sauce. So I added a couple of tablespoons of sour cream to the cheese and broccoli. Now, final experience proved Nigel Slater was right, and I could have had faith and left it the way it was. But I have to admit, that sour cream didn't hurt things. It could have been butter, instead, or cream, come to think of it.

When the pasta was tender but still had some bite to it—about ten minutes total—I drained it without shaking (to keep some of the cooking water) and added quickly to the pasta bowl with the warmed cheese and broccoli and etc. Tossed it all, melting the cheese even more in a very satisfying way. Turned it out into the two smaller warmed bowls, and served with lemon wedges and red pepper to shake on at table.

And it was great. But Nigel Slater was still right. Probably he was right about the five ounces of Gorgonzola per serving, too. One of these days I have to have faith and try it his way, too.

In the meantime, though, try it any way you feel like it, and I'll bet you'll still be very happy. We were. Though of course we're inclined to be happy at dinnertime. Which is not a bad thing.

Then, of course, there's broccoli and goat cheese with whole wheat pasta.

For two. For four, just double amounts.

Bring a huge pot of water to boil.

Peel a half-pound or so of broccoli (you don't have to do this, but I like to). Divide into flowerets, and quarter the stems.

Salt the water when it boils, dump the broccoli in. Cook till a moment past bright green—it should be tender. Scoop it out—SAVE THE WATER. Put the water back in the pot.

Bring water to the boil again. Add half a pound of whole wheat pasta (you can use regular pasta too, but whole wheat's best with this)—I recommend penne.

Chop the broccoli. Chop some garlic (I use lots—start with one clove and work up at will). Put a couple of tablespoons of olive oil in a wide skillet. If the garlic is old and dried, warm it in the oil till golden, then add the broccoli. If the garlic is new and juicy, just throw it in with the broccoli.

Dice up a 3 ounce or so goat cheese. Use anything you want, really. (I stole this idea from Marcella Hazan, and she uses Mozzarella.) Grate some Parmesan, too, if you have it.

Heat the broccoli and garlic gently. When the pasta is done, drain it—SAVE THE WATER—and add the drained, cooked pasta with the goat cheese and a ½ cup of the pasta water to the skillet. Cook medium high till the water evaporates, and the whole sauce is amalgamated and clinging to the pasta.

Serve in warmed bowls, with the grated Parmesan. Red pepper flakes are nice with this. And a simple salad after in the same bowl to mop up the sauce.

About the water you cooked the pasta and broccoli in—it makes a great soup base, too. Which makes you feel like you're improvising on a higher level altogether.

I can't remember where I got the recipe for Swiss Chard with Poblanos and Hominy. *Bon Appétit? Food and Wine? Gourmet?* Anyway, it's sitting there, taped in the back of a book I have jammed full of scrawled notes about dinners I've made, recipes I've liked, things to try, etc.

I can reconstruct why I probably clipped it in the first place. There's that can of hominy sitting dolefully in the back of my cupboard, bought in a rush of enthusiasm for vegetarian posole, something I couldn't seem to get right, until I discovered that canned hominy was the problem. Unmessed with canned hominy, it turns out, tastes like cardboard.

I probably clipped the recipe in hopes that I could use that last can up without too much pain sometime. I hate to waste food. Hate, hate, hate to waste food. Hate to waste anything, really, but food waste actually keeps me up nights; it seems like so much disrespect to where we came from and where we're going, if you know what I mean. So I know I was determined to eat that hominy.

I was determined to enjoy it, too. I can still remember the last time I put anything in my mouth that I didn't enjoy. It was during the dark days when I actually thought that racing around killing myself was somehow going to end in some glorious achievement— the days before I realized there was no more glorious achievement than enjoying your lunch and helping other people enjoy theirs. The Beloved Husband, who was similarly insane at the time, and I spent a lot of time on trains in the north of England. Even mentioning it makes my heart pound and the blood rush painfully to my head, as if I'm about to be late for the 9:35 to London, or the 11:12 to Bradford via Leeds. Anyway, before we ran onto the train (usually at the last minute), we would get our breakfast, or our lunch, or what would pass for our dinner, at one of the little sandwich places in the station. Plastic wrapped sarnies. Disgusting things. You eat them and you think, "The people who made these hate their jobs." I ate a lot of plastic wrapped sarnies over those dark years. Then, one day—I'm pretty sure it was on a train to Nottingham—I bit into a "Roasted Vegetable and Feta on Whole Meal Bread," and I thought to myself, "No." I thought, "I can't do this anymore." I thought, "I would rather be hungry than ever put one more calorie into my mouth that I don't thoroughly enjoy." I finished the sandwich—I told you I hate waste more than anything—then sat down to brood for the rest of the trip about how my life in general had gotten to be just like that sandwich. Something bolted quickly because the results were always going to be tomorrow. Something not enjoyed. Something everyone else around me did, too, with a similar grim sense of purpose. Something too expensive and just not worth it.

"Things," I thought as I considered, depressed, the food options of Nottingham where I would be spending the next ceremonial couple of days, "have got to change."

And they did. To my knowledge, I never ate a plastic wrapped sandwich ever again. And I realized that I wasn't helping the world one bit by racing around and hating my life. I realized I had better sit down and think all that through again. And I realized it was going to take some time.

In the meantime, I had to eat. And I was going to enjoy it, too.

All this to explain how I messed with that recipe for Chard and Poblanos and Hominy. I'd been to the market in between snowstorms and thrown with abandon into my cart whatever vegetables and fruits looked good and relatively inexpensive.

The Co-op was selling local organic collard greens in a huge, cheap bunch. I didn't worry what I'd do with them. I'd think of something. I was confident about that.

A few days later, for dinner, I felt like eating something Mexican, with some corn tortillas and an avocado/roasted tomato salad. I looked doubtfully at the collard greens. I don't think I'd ever cooked collard greens. I vaguely remembered Southern cooks braise hell out of them with various pork products. That sounded heavenly to me, but it wouldn't do for the Beloved Vegetarian Husband. So cook them with some chipotle chilies en adobo? Over garlic rice? I sighed. That didn't seem at all interesting just at the moment. I mean, it would on a different day, but just not now.

Then I remembered that recipe. It promised "Hominy turns roasted poblanos and Swiss chard into a hearty side dish." I mistrusted that "hearty" word. "Hearty" in my experience translates into "stodge." Also, reading the recipe, it asked me to roast a couple of poblanos, which I didn't have, and then cook them lightly with a red onion, which I also didn't have, some chard and garlic, and then add the hominy for one minute to heat through. Which would taste, I figured, like cardboard heated for one minute through.

It did suggest serving with lime wedges, though, which perked me up. I really think just about anything tastes good with lime juice and hot sauce on top.

So while I pottered around, I mulled the whole question over. I gave the Husband a particularly nice lunch so, if dinner failed, at least he'd have one good meal to look back on (reheated vegetable stew with re-baked leftover mashed potatoes covered with Swiss cheese on top). And I noticed I had a jar shoved in the back of the cupboard of fancy Mirasol roasted chilies. A house present from a very tasteful guest (thank you, Marjorie). Then, in the evening, I got to work deconstructing that recipe. Instead of "Swiss Chard with Poblanos and Hominy," it turned into "Collard Greens, Preserved Chilies and Hominy Hash." Damned good it was, too.

Here's how:

For four people, depending on side dishes, or for two people with leftovers for lunch the next day:

1 bunch of collard greens.

Soak these till clean of dirt. Strip tough stems away, shred the rest. Steam until tenderish. Don't worry if they stop being bright green; they're going to be a kind of grayish green by the time you've stewed them with everything else. They'll taste heavenly, though.

While you're steaming the greens . . .

In a big, wide skillet, sauté one thinly sliced onion. Let it get all browned and flavorful. When it has, add two chopped garlic cloves, two or three diced preserved chilies (canned Anaheim chilies would be just fine here if you didn't have a house guest who left you a jar of fancy roasted Mirasols), and a chipotle chile en adobo with a little of its sauce. (I recommend keeping a can of these around. When you've opened the can, just put the rest into a jar—they keep in the fridge for a long time.) Add some salt.

Add the steamed collards, and a little of their steaming liquid if things seem too dry. Cook over low heat so everything melds in flavor, at least five minutes—longer won't hurt it. Think of this as a kind of hash. The more it cooks together, the more the flavors mix—I cooked it about fifteen minutes. Just don't let it get too dry.

About ten minutes before you want to serve dinner, add a half a 29-ounce can drained hominy. More or less—eyeball it—to your own taste. That was mine. Freeze the rest to use in another dish. Don't worry too much about the cooking time, only you need to cook it at least till the hominy takes on some flavor. Ten minutes at least. It can cook longer, if you want it to. Or, you can always turn off the heat and reheat it when you call everyone to table, if that suits you better.

Salt to taste.

Put foil wrapped corn tortillas into a 350° oven to heat through—about ten minutes.

Serve the hash with the heated tortillas, lime wedges, hot sauce, and whatever salad you think would be nice scooped up with it in the tortillas. Shredded cabbage would be nice. Grated carrot. I had some roasted tomatoes in the fridge, so I diced a couple and tossed them with a diced avocado, chopped cilantro, a scallion, a squeeze of lime juice and some flax oil. That was great with it.

We're not huge eaters, so three tortillas apiece, and half the hash, along with the salad, were enough for us. But this dish would be great alongside some baked pork ribs, or carnitas, or even some Mexican baked chicken. Or on top of some garlic rice. I'd go for brown rice, myself. Better with the flavors.

And for lunch the next day, we had it warmed up again on top of shredded cabbage and grated carrot laid on heated whole wheat tortillas, with cilantro sprinkled on top and a dollop of sour cream. More lime wedges and hot sauce. Divine. And the hominy tasted like adobo sauce and garlic, not like cardboard at all.

Waste makes me anxious. Any kind of waste. Of course I come from a family that was made anxious by both the World War and the Depression—two good things to be anxious about—and as a result regarded waste as a kind of offering to the gods. If we waste stuff, you'll give us more, right?

As an adult, I can understand this and suffer along with the terror underneath shown by those overstuffed trash cans and overworked disposal units. I can still remember my mother urging me to take care of the jewelry she gave me, because I would be able to barter it for food when the next war came. I was amused by that when I was a child. Not anymore, though.

When I go back to my parents' house, the one thing I find hard to bear is how much food there is in the refrigerator . . . and then we go out to buy some more. And then we throw out food in the refrigerator to make room for the food we bought. And then we eat too much of everything. And then we throw more food out. And then we eat more. And then we complain about how much we ate, and then we talk about diets.

I love my family, but this just about drives me out of my mind.

I love my country, too. But it is just like my family in this. And it just about drives me out of my mind.

So the way I soothe this anxiety is that in the midst of my own and my country's abundance (for how long, I shiver and think, given all the waste . . . for how long?) . . . I make a small game with myself to use up every possible bit and bob I buy at the store. What we don't eat, the dogs get. What the dogs don't get goes on the compost heap. And so on. (I have a similar game whenever I leave the house for any length of time—making a last dinner for a friend of mine with whatever's left in the fridge. We've had some memorable and unexpected dinners, that way, and it's more than a little bit of fun.)

Soothing this week's anxiety: asparagus. They're everywhere; Mexico must be having a very good season. So I buy pounds of them, and store them upright in a yogurt container with a little water, like a bunch of flowers, on the top shelf of the refrigerator. And we eat them every known way: boiled and hot with olive oil, or melted butter, or just plain lemon. Room temperature with olive oil and lemon, or with soy sauce, sesame oil, lime juice, and toasted sesame seeds on top. Roasted in butter. With garlic mayonnaise. And so on.

I save the ends, those bits I snapped off idly before putting the spears on to cook. Those make a really good Asparagus Soup, one of my husband's favorite lunches, in fact.

Like so: When I have a good bag of them, from about two pounds of asparagus, I trim off the end woody bit (it's not very much, you'd be surprised), and give them a good soak in water. While that's happening, I mince a half an onion and sauté it in a tablespoon of butter. Then I throw in the cleaned asparagus ends. If I have an extra baked potato in the fridge, I skin it and dice it and throw that in. If not, I peel a raw potato and either dice it or grate it, and throw it in. Salt. Cover this with either water or vegetable juices you've prudently saved in a cleaned out apple juice jug in the fridge. (The water the asparagus spears cooked in the night before is perfect.) Simmer till the liquid is absorbed and the vegetables are tender. Throw the whole thing in the food processor or blender, or put through a food mill, and give it a couple of whirls.

When you're ready to serve it, put it back in the pan with a cup of milk and a cup of water or veg broth or any broth you have handy. Heat and simmer so flavors meld. Add two tablespoons of cream or sour cream, if you've got them, or a tablespoon of butter if you don't.

Serve with garlic rubbed toast and a little goat cheese. And then, as MFK Fisher says, you can say that you have dined.

(Above proportions are for two people—for four, just double.)

Every so often, you have an improvisation that you want to remember just because it made you and your companion stop and look at the plate and eat much more ssllllooowwwwllllllyy than usual. This happened the other night.

Normally, I would just think: ah, that parsley/cheese/pasta gambit worked, use it some other time . . . but this particularly parsley/cheese/pasta gambit was so harmonious on the plate that I wanted to write down EXACTLY HOW I DID IT so I won't forget.

The night in question, I'd wanted pasta. Mainly because, in the larder were: half a box of a nice eggy dried fettuccine, two of Dawn's eggs, and a handful of mushrooms. This seemed to cry out for mushroom carbonara.

But as the dinner hour approached, for some reason mushroom carbonara didn't appeal. It was too hot outside. I didn't feel like getting out the frying pan. I just wanted something that could be thrown together and tossed in the big pasta pot after the pasta was done. And I wanted something that involved lots and lots of parsley.

I often want something that involves lots and lots of parsley. So I have a tendency to remember recipes I come across that lean that way. While I was finishing up the day's duties, my mind drifted occasionally toward dinner. And a little marker popped up in my head: James Beard, it said.

So I went hunting, and then I found the recipe in his book on pasta: a brief description of an ultra simple sauce. A stick of butter melted with a clove of garlic. A bunch of parsley with a hunk of cheese processed together. All of it mixed with pasta at the last minute.

This sounded good. Just what I was looking for. And just vague enough so I could imagine riffs around it of just exactly what I wanted to cook and eat.

This is what you do for two people (for four, just double):

Put a big pot of pasta water on to boil.

Chop a huge, juicy, new clove of garlic and add to a small pan with half a stick of butter.

Put almost a whole bunch of parsley and one lone branch of fresh basil into a food processor with about 2 ounces of Gorgonzola and 2 ounces of domestic Parmesan. Process till a cheesy green mass.

Put half a pound of dried egg fettuccine into the boiling pasta water. Set timer.

Melt the butter gently around the garlic.

Drain the cooked pasta and mix with the melted butter and garlic, then with the mixed parsley and cheese. Toss thoroughly. Taste for salt and pepper and adjust to your liking.

Serve with a little grated Romano or Parmesan on the table.

Green salad for after, to mop up what's left on the plate. Dressing of pounded thyme leaves and a little garlic, pepper and salt, mixed with limejuice, walnut oil, and a touch of soy.

Glasses of a nice, cheerful, Spanish red wine.

Alex took one bite, looked at the plate in a mooning sort of way, and said, "This is a perfect dish of pasta. I'm going to eat this really sssllllloooowwwww."

So we did.

And then there's cold sorrel and potato soup.

First, either grow some sorrel or have a neighbor who does. It grows like a weed—in fact, the edible wild sorrel with which I sometimes make this soup IS a weed. Then buy the cheapest organic potatoes in the market that day. (They have to be organic because the sprouticide that industrial farms use to lengthen shelf life of conventional potatoes is not a thing you want in your or your loved ones' systems.) Buy a pound of organic onions (same thing applies as with the potatoes), or some other member of the edible lily family. Have on hand some cream or sour cream, and some other green herb to sprinkle, eventually on top. Parsley's fine, dill's nice, though I think chervil or chives are the best options.

Take about a pound of the potatoes and a pound of onions or leeks (or mixture of the two . . . or a bunch of scallions . . . or some shallots . . . you get the idea). Peel and slice or dice them. Put in a soup pot with about two quarts of water. Add a little salt. Cook till tender. Then add as much shredded sorrel (first having removed any tough stems) as you have. Cook till sorrel turns grayish green. (Don't worry—that's what it's supposed to do. It'll taste fine.)

At this point, you make a command decision. Either you leave it the way it is (comfortingly rustic), or you puree it (very elegant). You can do the latter by passing the soup through a food mill, or by putting it in the food processor. Many, many cookbooks have assured me that I should never put potatoes in the food processor— supposedly they become a "gluey mess"—but I have never had a problem with doing it this way for soups, so I say go with it.

When it cools, add a bit of cream or sour cream to taste—a quarter cup or so, erring on the side of generosity. (A half a cup would not be too much, in my opinion.) Salt to correct the seasoning. (Put the pepper mill on the table for people who want some.)

Chill the whole thing overnight.

Serve in chilled bowls or cups, sprinkled with fresh herbs. Other possible garnishes: thin slices of lemon. Or whipped salted cream sprinkled with some snipped chives. Or a little dab of sour cream with chopped dill.

Delicious. Simple. Frugal. Local. And—a bonus—good for you and your loved ones, too.

And the whole thing is just one lovely improvisation . . .

There's No Place Like Home

The first few days home after a gorge fest of any kind—a trip, say, to somewhere like Spain, where every meal comes with enormous amounts of delicious fried potatoes, pools of green thick olive oil, bottles of irresistible wine, and coffee with brandy to follow—we're both very inclined to high vegetable, low fat dishes of all kinds. (A frequent First Night Home meal is steamed broccoli on brown rice, which shows you how extreme the cure has to be.) So one of our favorite First Lunches At Home is a lentil and tuna salad with whole wheat pita bread. Easy. Delicious, too.

And this is how:

For four people (or two people with leftovers to be doctored into new freshness for another lunch):

One cup of lentils, preferably Puy lentils, which hold their shape. Pick over for stones and rinse. (Don't skip this step. Every so often I get cocky and do skip it, and I always regret it when somebody finds a rock in their soup. So to be careful, I let the lentils run slowly through my fingers into a colander, eyeing them closely for foreign objects as they go.)

Put lentils in a pot with an unpeeled garlic clove and bay leaf, cover with a little water—about up to the first knuckle of your finger, if your finger rests on the top of the lentils. Bring to boil, turn down

183

heat but still cook briskly.

Meanwhile, dice a carrot. Add that as you finish dicing, to cook with the lentils.

Now put in a salad bowl:
Two stalks peeled and thinly sliced celery.
Two sliced scallions.
As much chopped parsley as you like.
A tablespoon of rinsed and chopped capers.
A can's worth of drained, flaked tuna.

Make the dressing:
1 garlic clove mashed with pepper and salt. 1 tablespoon sherry vinegar. 3 or 4 tablespoons olive oil.

When lentils are tender—after about 20 to 30 minutes; if there is too much liquid, boil it down rapidly or drain it, but probably you won't have much left at this point—add them to salad bowl and toss with the dressing. Correct the seasoning, as they say . . .

Serve on a bed of mesclun lettuce, or shredded other lettuce, with warmed whole wheat pita breads to scoop up.

If we eat that, both of us drinking water and reading our various luncheon reading materials, even though we both think it was great walloping through a week's worth of wine and olive oil soaked meals, we know in our hearts it's even greater to be home . . .

(. . . and for lunch the next day, I added fresh grated carrot and mesclun lettuce to what was left, tossed it all together and served it with

warmed whole wheat tortillas, with lemon halves on the side to brighten it up. Even thinking about that lunch makes me glad to be home all over again.)

Did I mention I like coming home?

After, say, two weeks of questionable food values taken in at a variety of restaurants (don't get me wrong, some of those questionable food values can taste awfully good . . . but still . . .), it's always a pleasure to be back at the stove. We eat a lot of vegetables before we get back to feeling halfway normal. Of course the first, easiest, most comforting dish to eat in those circumstances is vegetable soup. Like this:

Melt a tablespoon of butter over low heat in a medium sized pan. Mince an onion and sauté it until it's soft. Meanwhile, dice a carrot, a stalk of celery, and a potato. Add them and 1 teaspoon of curry powder (or to taste) to the onion. Sauté for a bit while you slice a few mushrooms, mince some parsley, maybe dice a summer squash. Whatever veggies you have about—a turnip is nice, in which case, add with the potato. Add the other veggies. Salt. Add about three cups of water, a little white wine if you have some open, and simmer for about a half hour, till the vegetables are done and have traded flavors with the soup. Taste for seasoning. Serve with toast, or croutons, or a piece of toast with melted cheese floated in the bowl.

There should be enough for 4 moderate eaters, but since we're immoderate, there's usually about one serving left. But no problem. For example, the next night, we had baked potatoes, creamed chard, gingered carrots, and tomato salad. I baked the potatoes alongside a big pan of apples sprinkled with brown sugar and a little water in the pan. The apples, cooled down, were my breakfast the rest of the week—sometimes with cream, sometimes with yogurt . . . depended on the day. The leftover potato peels went into the dog's food. The leftover potatoes got mashed with garlic and cream and covered with shredded Swiss cheese, for the start of a dinner later week.

And for lunch the day after *that*—I added the water that I used to steam the chard and the carrots for dinner the night before to the one helping of leftover soup. Then I added the leftover creamed chard. I cooked that for awhile to mingle flavors. Serve with butter sautéed croutons—the last of the bread.

As MFK Fisher says, and now I know I've *dined*.

Then there's how good it is to get home after a rather intense day. We had one that included our little dog biting the chunk out of the ear of a dog he was being introduced to at the pound as a possible pal. True, the other dog started it, but it still was embarrassing, as you can imagine. When we got home, I just wanted to have a glass of red wine and something very easy to cook and easy to eat. Something basic. Something involving Dawn's eggs and the just out of the oven whole wheat sourdough I bought from the bread truck in the store parking lot before the guy even wheeled the bread in. But

I didn't just want eggs. When I feel a trifle stressed, I always want cheese. Apparently, this is common: we want full fat when we feel down. I don't know why the full fat I always crave at these times is either really aged Cheddar or Gorgonzola, but as a neighbor of mine once theorized "That's because even when you're stressed, you're still discriminating about your cheeses."

Nice theory, anyway.

I thought about Welsh Rabbit, but I didn't want to make anything with beer, and it seemed like too much hoopla.

Another parameter: I had these nice asparagus, which I really wanted to eat as salad.

(*I've discovered that the near perfect dressing for asparagus is white truffle oil, a sprinkling of flaked salt, and a big spritz of lemon juice. You dress the hot spears the minute they come off the stove, and let them sit till you're ready to eat, occasionally basting them with their own juices. Really fabulous. The white truffle oil, of course, was a gift from a dear friend a Christmas or two ago, and I puzzled over it for some time before realizing that this was the use it was meant for.*)

What would go with the asparagus, on the same plate, so the dressing running under whatever it was would add to its taste, rather than making me wonder why everything was so soggy? Using, might I add, a wonderfully aged Tillamook Cheddar, eggs, and some sourdough whole wheat bread?

As often happens when I narrow it down like this, I found the answer while browsing in the indexes of cookbooks.

(*This, mind you, is my way of winding down after putting the groceries away—I figure out which books are closest to the style of how I feel like eating, then I get my glass of wine, and go sit in my big armchair with a stack of my cookbook picks on the ottoman, reading my way through and considering and discarding various possibilities before I figure out which one is closest to what I want. Then, when I've got a little guidance, I begin the fascinating process of modifying it further to the circumstances. I know, I know, it sounds like a daft hobby, but, as I point out to my film mad husband, who knows everything there is to know about spaghetti westerns, my way of relaxing does result in something good to eat.)*

This time I found what I wanted in a Deborah Madison cookbook. I go to her, and to Marion Cunningham, when I want something sensible and straightforward and delicious. I can count on them. They both give the strong impression of being just the woman you would want living next door when your husband's having a midnight heart attack, or your daughter's about to give premature birth, or a bat's got into the attic. That's the way they both read. I trust them.

Anyway, Deborah Madison did not let me down. She had, in her index, something called "Baked Cheese on Toast," and when I got there, I found it was pretty much what I wanted, except for using Gruyere rather than Cheddar. So big deal, I just substituted, and added a couple of dashes of hot sauce, too.

This was how, for the two of us.

Preheat the oven to 400°. Lightly beat two eggs, add two cups grated sharp Cheddar, and a quarter cup of white wine. Add a dash or two of hot sauce. Spread on four pieces of rather thickly cut bread, whole wheat sourdough for choice. Paprika the top, if you've got any paprika handy.

In a pan big enough to hold all the bread flat, melt 2 tablespoons of butter. (I do this by just shoving the pan into the oven as it heats up; by the time I've mixed everything else the oven is hot and the butter is melted.) Then swirl in the pan another quarter cup of white wine. Lay the bread in the pan, and bake till the cheese melts, about 12 minutes.

Serve on the same plate with asparagus dressed with white truffle oil and lemon juice. Another wedge of lemon on the side does not come amiss.

Any kind of wine you fancy—I had red, the Husband had rosé.

No muss, no fuss. And we laughed while we ate, and decided our dog was going to have to be an only dog for a little while longer—at least until they'd forgotten about his disgraceful behavior at the pound.

Then there was the night a board meeting for the local fire department ran overtime, and all the way home my brain seethed with plans for a quick platter of eggs (creamy scrambled with white wine and garlic), warmed whole wheat tortillas, sliced avocado and lettuce leaves with lime. I could have that on the table in fifteen minutes, even allowing for careful maneuvering around the dog.

But when I got home, I really, really wanted to sit down with a glass of wine first, and tell the Beloved Husband all the gossip I'd picked up at the fire meeting. And if I was going to sit down anyway . . . then I remembered the two Portobello mushrooms still tucked away in the fridge.

I love Portobello mushrooms. There's one store around here that sells them relatively cheaply, and whenever I'm in there I buy enough for a couple of meals. They were a huge hit at a carnivorous Thanksgiving dinner I made for my brother and sister in law and their kids—my nephew and niece ate everything in sight, and very satisfyingly said that the vegetables were the best part. I stuffed the mushrooms that time, which is kind of gilding the lily, though easy enough.

(For 2 mushrooms, about a half cup bread crumbs tossed till golden in a skillet with a good wodge of butter, chopped garlic, chopped scallions or shallots, lots of chopped parsley, the minced stalks of the mushrooms, a little cream or sour cream or mayonnaise to bind—if I make four or more mushrooms, I increase the stuffing and add a beaten egg to bind the whole thing, but with the smaller amount of stuffing these others work fine—, salt, pepper, baste the mushroom caps in melted butter, stuff, bake them at 375° for about thirty minutes, or at whatever you've got everything else in at until they're done. . .)

Easy. Not easy enough, though.

This is the easiest way to cook Portobello mushrooms. And it may be the best. It's a tweaked idea of Nigel Slater's, and this is how it goes: in a dish big enough to hold the mushrooms, put them upside down. (Leave the stalks on, though you must trim off the dirty bits at the bottom. Our dogs love those cooked in their food later.) Chop a garlic clove or two and sprinkle in each. Dot generously with butter, about a tablespoon—if not more—for each. Then splash in a good capful of balsamic vinegar. More if you like it. Salt. Shove in a 400° oven for twenty, twenty-five, minutes. Baste every so often if you think of it, but you don't need to be fanatical about it. If you're comfortable sitting on the couch, don't bother getting up, is what I mean. They'll taste just fine anyway.

Not only are they delicious, but they smell great while they're cooking. Always an added bonus, I think. And they gave me an extra fifteen minutes to put my feet up, before I went back to the kitchen to put the tortillas in to warm, and cook the eggs—a ½ cup of white wine with chopped garlic and a tablespoon of butter cooked on high heat till it reduced down to a few tablespoons, then taken off the heat to let cool. Then I cracked eggs into it, put on LOW heat, gave it a stir, halfway into cooking add Swiss cheese in a small dice, when almost done added a handful of chopped parsley, salt and pepper to taste. Poured onto warmed tortillas when the eggs were as creamy as I liked, taking care not to overcook—sliced the avocado, piled it on lettuce leaves, spritzed lime over all and added extra lime wedges to the plates. Put the mushrooms nestled up on the lettuce leaves.

That done, I poured myself another glass of wine, and we sat down to eat. And it felt like a luxuriously leisurely dinner, rather than one rushed because I got home too late. I think that might have been the mushrooms. And they were so easy, too.

So I was home after Christmas, full up to here with cooking and eating and watching the levels of the See's candy boxes drop radically between the hours of six and nine p.m., and I wanted to make something for dinner that didn't exactly say, "It's the end of the holidays and I'm sick of them," but didn't exactly say, "I never want the holidays to end," either.

The perfect solution was potato soup.

Of course I always have potatoes. And so do you, if it's after Christmas. Don't tell me you didn't get in a five or ten pound bag for the inevitable mashed extravaganza. I know you did.

So. If it is after Christmas, and you and your digestive system are tired out with partying, do what I did: get on the phone to have a chat with some friend who was too busy on the day itself to talk. Prop the phone between shoulder and chin. And get chopping.

For four people:

A blurb of butter in a big pot—about 2 tablespoons. Melt gently.

Mince an onion, a big stalk of celery, a little parsley, and three or four or five potatoes—depending on size and your own capacity. Add the onion and celery and parsley to the butter. Crumble in some thyme, dried or fresh; add a bay leaf and some salt and pepper.

Cook gently till onion is opaque. Add a cup of water. Cook, still gently, for about ten minutes.

Add potatoes, and another little bit of water—about a half cup. Cover and cook for another ten minutes. Then add 2 cups of milk and cook till it's all falling apart in the pan.

Let cool for a moment (this is your opportunity to stop saying, "mm-hmm, mm-hmm, mm-hhmm, he DIDN'T! What did you do then?" and take over the conversation for a time while your friend does some chore on her end and listens to YOU.)

Put some of the chunky vegetables through a food mill, if you have one, or in a blender, or just mash them into the soup with a potato masher. Add back to the pot with a half-cup of cream, if you have it.

Correct seasoning.

When you're ready to serve, say good-bye to your friend, hang up the phone, and then heat soup gently back to steaming.

Serve with toast and Gorgonzola cheese. The Husband crumbles the cheese into his soup and then makes contented noises all the way till the salad.

(Did I mention the salad? It's particularly good with this soup with a lemon/thyme/garlic dressing.)

Afterwards, you might even feel enough courage to face the tin of candied walnuts and ginger shortbread. I generally force myself. After all, it's that time of year.

I can't be the only one who arrives at the holidays to the parental home and finds herself unable to stop eating cookies, candies, cakes and various festive oils, butters, meats, as well as a staggering variety of carbohydrates. Something about the Great Return always involves a great lowering of the fruit and vegetable intake. Now this is very pleasant. There's nothing like a cookie with a picture of Santa somehow mysteriously implanted right in its very center eaten right after a leftover pot roast sandwich. Or even before it. But coming home to one's own normal habits, well, that's something of a relief to the stomach and the central nervous system after all that celebrating generally. You have to heal up from the holidays. If you can find time to do this in their very midst, so much the better.

Here is one of my holiday healing meals, generally taken the very day I come back to my own dear home:

Steamed broccoli.

Added butter, soy sauce, Thai hot sauce, and squeezed lemon to taste.

Then, in the evening, feeling virtuous and like I might be easing back into my normal groove, I often notice that there is, say, a pint of milk left over from the week before in the fridge. Likely to go bad. And I'm usually quite hyped up after trips, and don't sleep my usual sleep of the just. So I make Hot Milk and Honey and sip it by the fire, with the dogs snoring soporifically at my feet.

Here's how:

First, and this is perhaps the most important part of the recipe, pick your mug. This should be a wide, thick walled mug, the one that reminds you the most of the most pleasant days—fantasized or otherwise—of childhood. I have two or three I eye at these moments. For some reason, they all have rather goofy flowers on their sides.

Now heat your milk. Add a spoonful of honey and a glog of vanilla. Then, right when a bubble or two begins to appear, and it starts to steam, add a glup of heavy cream and a capful of Irish whiskey. Pour into your mug. Take your mug to a strategic position where you can enjoy it in peace.

Whenever I do this, I'm glad to be home. And the dogs are glad I am, too.

There is, after all, no place like it anywhere else in the whole wide world.

Postscript
Cavalho Cancado

I notice there are a couple of recipes I mention that I don't actually share in the body of the book. The most important one of these is my favorite bizarre heritage dish, "Cavalho Cancado," translated by my Macanese grandmother as "Tired Horses." This sounds absolutely awful, and doesn't exactly look like something you'd see on the cover of *Gourmet*.

But trust me. People love them. Teenagers, especially, have been known to down dozens at a time.

They are, in theory anyway, canapés for a party—though I was known, in my college years, to make big pieces of them to eat for my dinner. So, again in theory, you put the meat mixture on top of whatever size bits of bread you like. My grandmother always used triangles cut from horrible store bought white bread, and as long as the bread was stale, they tasted terrific. My own college years refinement was to use sourdough bread, which I prided myself on as an improvement, once I'd realized that you HAD to use stale bread or suffer the consequences. I would just dry out what pieces of bread I had in the oven, and then cut them into pretty rounds with a cookie cutter.

Here's the original, and slightly enigmatic, recipe, as it came down to me, scrawled in my teenage handwriting, from my grandmother:

"Cavalho Cancado"
(Tired Horses, but it's not as romantic)

      Ground chuck
      1 tblspn. Flour, 1 egg per lb.
      3 swirls of shoyu per 2lb.
      green onions
      1 tsp. of sugar per 2 lb.
      1 swirl of vinegar per 2 lb.

      325° ½ hour

Here's the interpretation:
For every pound of ground hamburger, add a tablespoon of flour, an egg, a couple of swirls of soy sauce (I always added more than the recipe), chopped scallions, a ½ teaspoon of sugar, and at least a swirl of red wine vinegar. Mix. *(I used my hands. And why not?)* Adjust seasoning.

Dry out some bread in a 200° oven, till it's dried but not brown. Cut into whatever shapes appeal to you. Spread some of the ground meat mixture on each piece, put canapés on cookie sheets. Cook as directed above.

Honestly, if you're not a vegetarian, you won't be able to resist these. Or maybe even if you are.

As for my paella recipe, that'll just have to wait . . .

On My Bookshelf

Everything by MFK Fisher.
Everything by Elizabeth David.

Then, among others, alphabetical by author (because it's impossible to list in order of enjoyment):

Andoh, Elizabeth. *At Home with Japanese Cooking*. Alfred A. Knopf, 1980.

Beard, James. *The New James Beard*. Alfred A. Knopf, 1981.

———. *American Cookery*. Little, Brown, 1972.

Bittman, Mark. *The Best Recipes in the World*. Broadway Books, 2005.

Child, Julia. *From Julia Child's Kitchen*. Gramercy Books, 1975.

Cunningham, Marion (with Jeri Laber). *The Fannie Farmer Cookbook, Twelfth Ed.* Alfred A. Knopf, 1979.

Gin, Margaret. *Regional Cooking of China*. 101 Productions. 1977.

Hazan, Marcella. *Marcella Cucina*. Harper Collins. 1977.

Hopkinson, Simon. *Gammon and Spinach*. Macmillan,1998.

Hopkinson, Simon (with Lindsey Bareham). *Roast Chicken and Other Stories*. Hyperion, 2006.

Jaffrey, Madhur. *World Vegetarian*. Ebury Press, 1998.

Kennedy, Diana. *My Mexico*. Clarkson Potter, 1998.

Luard, Elisabeth. *The Old World Kitchen*. The Akadine Press, 1998.

Madison, Deborah. *Vegetarian Cooking for Everyone*. Broadway Books, 1997.

————. *The Savory Way*. Broadway Books, 1990.

Olney, Richard. *Simple French Food*. Macmillan, 1974.

De Pomiane, Edouard. *Cooking with Pomiane*. North Point Press, 1994.

Roberts, Michael. *Parisian Home Cooking*. William Morrow, 1999.

Ross, Janet (with Michael Waterfield). *Leaves from our Tuscan Kitchen*. Penguin Books, 1997.

Shulman, Martha Rose. *Provençal Light*. William Morrow, 1994.

Sigal, Jane. *Backroad Bistros, Farmhouse Fare*. Doubleday, 1994.

Slater, Nigel. *Appetite*. Clarkson Potter, 2000.

————. *Real Fast Food*. Penguin Books, 1992.

Thorne, John. *Simple Cooking*. Penguin Books, 1989.

Thorne, John (with Matt Lewis Thorne). *Serious Pig*. North Point Press, 1996.

Wells, Patricia. *Bistro Cooking*. Kyle Cathie Ltd, 1999.

Wolfert, Paula. *Mediterranean Grains and Greens*. Harper Collins, 1998.

Zelayeta, Elena. *Elena's Secrets of Mexican Cooking*. Prentice-Hall, Inc., 1969.

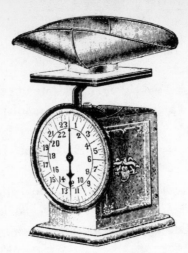

Temperatures, Weights, and some Measures

It's more usual in American cookbooks—even ones like this—for recipe measurements to be pretty precise. You've probably noticed that this book positively bubbles with imprecision. There isn't a recipe in here that can't be changed (and has been, as a matter of fact) in a fit of exuberance, or boredom, or of noticing you don't actually have some of the ingredients listed. That's the way I like to cook. Once in awhile it's fun to cook very precisely and specifically, with special ingredients added (and there are some cookbooks that really reward that method—anything by Julia Child and Richard Olney springs immediately to mind, among others). But generally, my feeling is that cooking is about knowing what you've got and what you like to do with it. For that kind of cooking, too much emphasis on precise measurements is not just beside the point, sometimes it downright gets in the way.

However. That said, you also need the friendly support of lists of ingredients, and measurements of ingredients, to act at least as a benchmark from which to judge your own efforts . . . at least, that's how I think of recipes when I read them, for pleasure or for information.

All of the measurements and temperatures in *Jam Today* are American ones, which means if you're cooking in the United Kingdom, and you want to use these as a guide, you have to make some adjustments. To give you an idea of what the equivalences are, more or less, I've listed a few here that I hope will be helpful—at least, they have been for me, who's spent some time cooking in both places.

Temperature

212 F = 100 C
225 F = 110 C
250 F = 130 C = Gas ½
275 F = 140 C = Gas 1
300 F = 150 C = Gas 2
325 F = 170 C = Gas 3

350 F = 180 C = Gas 4
375 F = 190 C = Gas 5
400 F = 200 C = Gas 6
425 F = 220 C = Gas 7
450 F = 230 C = Gas 8
475 F = 240 C = Gas 9

Weights

These are approximate. But in all the places I've used ounces—"oz."—, a little more or less in the gram—"g."—area won't really matter...

½ oz. = 10 g.

1 oz. = 25 g.

2 oz. = 50 g.

3 oz. = 100 g.

5 oz. = 150 g.

9 oz. = 250 g.

10 oz. = 300 g.

14 oz. = 400 g.

1 lb. = 450 g.

1 lb., 1½ oz. = 500 g.

Butter, Shortening, Cheese, and Other Fats

1 tbsp. = ⅛ stick = ½ oz. = 15 g.

2 tbsp. = ¼ stick = 1 oz. = 30 g.

4 tbsp. = ½ stick. = 2 oz = 60 g. = ¼ cup

8 tbsp. = 1 stick = 4 oz. = 115 g. = ½ cup

16 tbsp. = 2 sticks = 8 oz. = 225 g. = 1 cup

32 tbsp. = 4 sticks = 16 oz. = 450 g. = 2 cups

The easiest way to remember, for me, how to convert grams to ounces, is to think that an American pound of pasta—sixteen ounces—is a little less than the equivalent English package of 500 grams. So an English package gives a slightly more lavish result than an American package. Then I work back from there.

Index

Index

TOD DAVIES, passionate home cook and omnivore, thinks if you want the world to be a better place, you should start by making sure everyone is well fed. She lives in the mountains of Oregon with her vegetarian husband and two carnivorous dogs.